Celestial Navigation

Celestial Navigation

A Practical Guide

ARTHUR E. DAVIES

Helmsman Books

First published in 1992 by
Helmsman Books, an imprint of
The Crowood Press Ltd
Ramsbury, Marlborough
Wiltshire SN8 2HR

British Library Cataloguing in Publication Data

A catalogue record for this book is available from the British
Library.

ISBN 1 85223 679 5

Docendo Discimus

Picture credits

Line-drawings by Claire Upsdale-Jones
Figs 40, 43–8, 62–7, 70–6 © Terry Day
Figs 22–8 by Chris Dangerfield.

Typeset by Avonset, Midsomer Norton, Avon
Printed in Great Britain by Redwood Press Ltd, Melksham

Contents

Preface

When Vivaldi produced *The Four Seasons*, the gyrations of the heavenly bodies that cause them were contributing to the arts. In this book I show how they also serve science, using the elegance and predictability of their movements to establish the techniques of celestial navigation. A successful sight gives the curious feeling that these remote bodies recognize our need and temporarily devote themselves to us.

The position-fixing and route-finding practices which follow are relatively simple, and the equipment needed readily available. However, it was not so until comparatively recently.

The efforts of the ancients to find the size of the earth and seek their way about it seem absurd now, but, as a friend once remarked, they had no idea how long ago they were then living! What was needed was accurate time, accurate angular measuring devices and the ability to put it all together, with a sound knowledge of what was going on up there in the heavens. Progress is never steady, however. It comes in inspired spurts from gifted and dedicated individuals. Motivation is as much by intellectual curiosity as by military or commercial pressures.

The planets, the 'wandering stars', gave most problems of understanding. In the sixteenth century Kepler sorted them out. As an idealist, he wanted them to move in perfect circles but found himself proving that their motion was elliptical, and his three laws stating this were a triumph of the times. Kepler's studies were compromised by odd diversions, such as providing astrological fortune-telling for his court patrons, and occasionally rescuing his mother from being burned as a witch! When Tycho Brahe, the Danish astronomer, died, Kepler had no qualms over appropriating his experimental data, and he made a very rough coach trip to Italy for talks with Galileo, who was having his own problems with the Vatican. It was 1835 before the Church accepted the movements of heavenly bodies which these scientists had discovered. The problem of accurate time measurement, which is essential to derive longitude, was solved by chronometers, principally Harrison's. This influenced the situation where warring navies were stalking each other and wondering where they all were!

Of course, developing knowledge needed mathematical processing to be useful, not only to solve the navigational spherical triangle, but also to meet the needs of merchants dealing in shares and compounded interest. Thus were born the magic tools of logarithms and calculus. So there is much to philosophize about during a quiet night at sea when the stars are brilliant and you have, perhaps, been using a computer with the ephemeris for umpteen years in it.

The navigational bodies available to us are: the Sun and the Moon; the planets Venus, Mars, Jupiter and Saturn; plus about fifty stars. A sextant shot requires a horizon. When shooting the Sun, if the weather is fair enough for the sight, the horizon comes with it, so it is a 'user-friendly' body. The other bodies are shot in twilight (Civil Twilight q.v.) which adds interest and allows a direct fix if several bodies are shot at virtually the same time.

Celestial navigation theory is not difficult, but a few unusual concepts have to be grasped. If we persevere in following a Sun shot in rigorous detail, the rest will fall into place.

Introduction

The watershed created by the advent of electronic navigation has produced something of a dilemma amongst two groups of sailors, for whom this book might be a help.

First, there are those who have practised sextant/tables navigation, and who now enjoy the ease of electronic navigation, but who have an unease about their ability to pick the former up again at short notice if needed. They have just gone rusty. What better than a flowchart of the steps and a concise summary to bring it all back? This book offers that.

Second, there are those who have opted directly for electronic navigation and become a little nervous at the extended voyages they are now making without the back-up capability to use sextant/tables if needed. This group includes those who simply have not had time to attend astro-navigation courses. This book offers a 'working instruction' for the easiest and most commonly used practice of shooting the Sun and working a noon position.

Part One functions therefore as an *aide-mémoire* and a teaching system. To this end material which it is desirable to cover, but which would compromise the flow of Part One, is dealt with in later parts. Part Two amplifies the theory and deals with other techniques. Part Three covers the 'other' celestial bodies: the Moon, planets and stars. You are sometimes buying clarity at the cost of repetition.

How to Use This Book

If you need just a reminder, go through the flowcharts (Figs 1 and 2, *see* pages 11 and 12) and the summary of Part One (*see* page 69), which gives essential vocabulary, and the sequence of steps through *Reed's Almanac* and the Tables, to the plotting sheet entries. Those attending shore-based courses might find the outlined strategy useful. If you are totally new to this game, browse through Part One when you are relaxed and not under pressure. There is nothing more off-putting than a recitative and aria on this subject which takes too much on board too soon. You can, of course,

INTRODUCTION

recognize where passages contain material you can skip. It is unusual, however, for students not to feel attracted to the subject intellectually and be interested in its history. Refer to the flowcharts frequently, work through the examples, and be prepared to go back a bit at times.

Get the feel of the sextant early on. Practise 'rocking' to obtain the true vertical – the minimum reading for a given setting. You can use it indoors to bring a light, for example, down to a horizontal surface, such as a table top. Check the index error on the roof of a far building – it doesn't need be a horizon for practice. Remember that 'on the arc' is easy; 'off the arc' means you are approaching zero from below, so minus 4' actually reads 56' on the scale. Use on an opportunity basis on coastal and offshore trips. Get others to check readings and work through the Almanac and Tables, and then check your position line (PL) with your dead reckoning or deduced reckoning (DR). On most passages there are periods of enforced idleness and there are few better ways of using this time.

If the above remarks mean nothing to you at this stage, then be patient and come back later.

Part One: The Sun Sight

Setting the Scene

Flowchart A (Fig 1) is a pictorial outline of the consecutive steps. Flowchart B (Fig 2) takes this further to a notional sight at mid-afternoon in the Northern Hemisphere. These charts form an anchor to the text. The mechanical steps are straightforward and can be done by rote, but we need to understand the principles, which are tackled at 'notional' and 'working' levels.

First, regard a sight as a step towards *refining* your estimated position, your dead reckoning or deduced reckoning (DR). The system requires you to assume such a position as a basis for the calculations. One sight gives you a position line (PL), and you are somewhere on this line at the time of sight. The angle of the

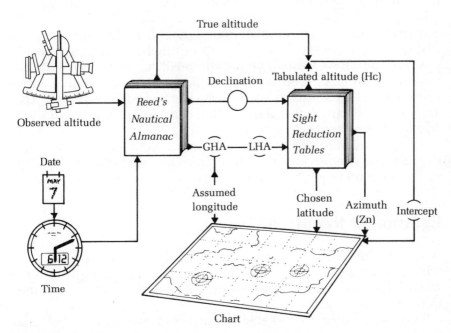

Fig 1   Flowchart A.

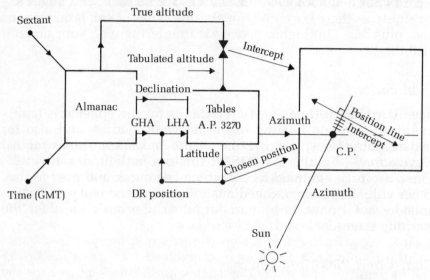

Fig 2 Flowchart B.

position line from a given body changes with time, so, after a while, you can take another sight and cross the position lines to get a fix. The first position line is transferred to the second by the course and distance run, as in standard coastal 'running fix' plots. On an ocean passage you thus establish your daily position. But a sun sight can also be useful on coastal or offshore passages, mixed with position lines from other sources, such as the radio-direction finder (RDF) and visual bearings. It is a marvellous and satisfying capability to add to your armoury.

Let us tackle the celestial navigation problem and its solution in the notional way; to grasp the principles and understand the terms in the flowcharts which might be new to you.

Equipment Required

A sextant, of course, is needed, as is a decent digital watch, for which you need to know the 'rate', that is the gain (usually) in seconds per week from time checks. An analogue watch is difficult to read accurately and quickly.

You need normal chart instruments and I suggest a dedicated Sight Book plus graph paper and/or plotting sheets. It is useful to record your height of eye from stations in the yacht you might use for sights, as there is a correction for this. The cockpit is an obvious one, plus one a bit higher if swell is interfering with your horizon visibility.

Publications

Reed's Nautical Almanac (1991): this is for the ephemeris (ephemerides); the data relating to the heavenly bodies, and also for sextant corrections. A.P. 3270 – *Sight Reduction Tables for Air Navigation* – Volume 3 (HMSO): this covers latitudes 40°–89°. These are pre-computed tables which are quick and easy to use. Other volumes are mentioned later. These can be replaced by calculators but I have to be fairly rigid on the basic tools for the learning stages.

Charts and Pictorial Drawings

You will be familiar with standard charts on Mercator projections where the parallels of latitude are horizontal and meridians of longitude are vertical. The longitude scales close up with increase in latitude, being equal at the equator. (Actually, it is the latitude scale that expands – same effect.) We shall be looking at global illustrations where latitude/longitude and their celestial equivalents, declination and hour angle, are great circles. These are shown as curves, the planes of which pass through the centre of the Earth. When we discuss these, be assured that the final plot of the position line is done on a standard chart or plotting sheet, in Mercator form.

Terms Used in the Flowcharts

Azimuth (Az.)   The bearing of a body, directly or indirectly, given in the *Sight Reduction Tables* (*see* 'The Mysteries of Z and Zn', page 37).

Chosen position (CP)   Your DR position rounded to the nearest whole degree of latitude, and whole degree of LHA. This allows the pre-computed Tables (Á.P. 3270) to operate.

Dead reckoning position (DR)   Your best estimate of the yacht's latitude/longitude position at the time the sight is taken. Usually extrapolated by course and distance run from the last known position.

Declination (Dec.)   Celestial latitude, north or south, found in the Almanac for navigational bodies (*see* Fig 3).

THE SUN SIGHT

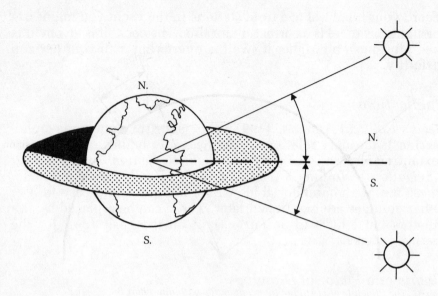

Fig 3   Declination.

Greenwich hour angle (GHA)   Measured up to 360° westward from the Greenwich meridian to the meridian of the body. This is found in the Almanac for any navigational body, for a precisely given time.

Hour angle   This measures longitude difference – meridian to meridian.

Intercept   The spacing of the difference between True Altitude and Tabulated Altitude along the azimuth from the chosen position.

Local hour angle (LHA)   Obtained by applying ship's longitude to GHA, subtracting if in west longitude, adding if in east longitude.

Tabulated altitude (Tab. Alt.)   Calculated from Tables. In A.P. 3270 it is expressed as Hc (height calculated).

True altitude (True Alt.)   Sextant altitude corrected for standard errors.

To comprehend these terms we also need to define a few which do not appear directly in the charts:

Geographical position (GP)   The point on the Earth's surface directly beneath a navigational body, expressed as declination and hour angle. The heavenly equivalents of latitude and longitude.

Zenith (Zen.)   The opposite; a notional point directly overhead.

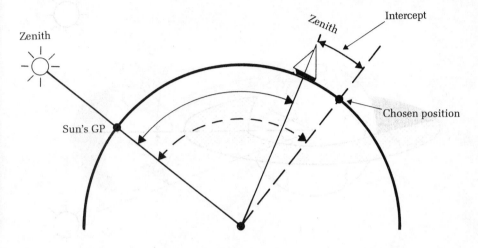

Fig 4   The Principle of St Hilaire Intercept (study with Flowchart B).

1. We can identify co-ordinates of the Sun's geographical position, *but cannot plot it*, so we cannot directly measure back from it.
2.   We can define the co-ordinates of a local position (CP) and plot it. We can calculate its distance from the Sun's geographical position. (Tab. Alt.).
3.   We can measure, with the sextant, the distance – yacht to Sun's geographical position (True Alt.).
4.   The difference between these two figures is the *intercept*, which is expressed in nautical miles, and allows us to plot from the chosen position to the yacht's true position. (This can be *to* or *from* the CP.) These motions are along a common bearing called the azimuth. The word intercept is used in the following sense: 'To mark off a certain space between two points or lines' (*OED*).

Distance: We need to compare two 'distance numbers' to derive the intercept. The sextant measures the altitude of the body above the horizon and its complement (90° minus Alt.) would be distance as shown in Fig 4 but there is no point in making this conversion because the calculated distance can be expressed as equivalent altitude. So we compare tabulated altitude with true sextant altitude.

15

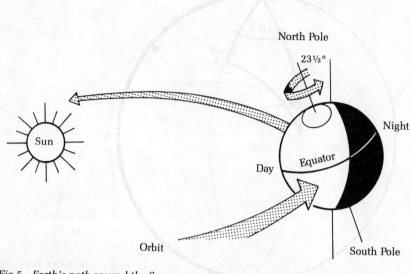

Fig 5   Earth's path around the Sun.

Taking and Plotting a Sun Sight – A Synopsis

We can use the two flowcharts, shown in Figs 1 and 2, and also Figs 6 and 7 to attempt this broad brush approach. No section of this book is more important. The geometric problem is shown in Fig 6.

Flowchart A (Fig 1)

Note that we start with a sextant reading and the precise time of observation, in GMT. Then there are paths through the Almanac and *Sight Reduction Tables*, concluding with the data we plot on the chart, or plotting sheet, to give the position line. One observation: one position line. The yacht was at some point on this line at the time of sight. You can identify two parallel paths leading to the sextant altitude and tabulated altitude which we compare to get the intercept, as shown in Fig 7.

Flowchart B (Fig 2)

If you regard the chart as oriented 'north up', the notional Sun appears in the south-west. It is mid-afternoon, local time, in the Northern Hemisphere. The chosen position has been plotted; the

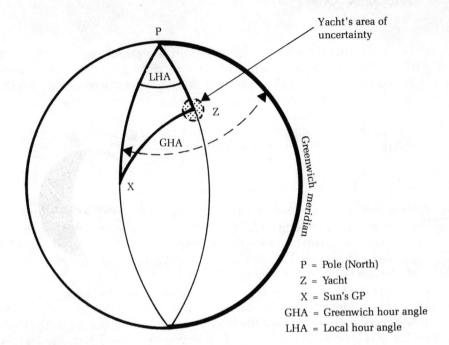

P = Pole (North)
Z = Yacht
X = Sun's GP
GHA = Greenwich hour angle
LHA = Local hour angle

Fig 6   The PZX triangle.

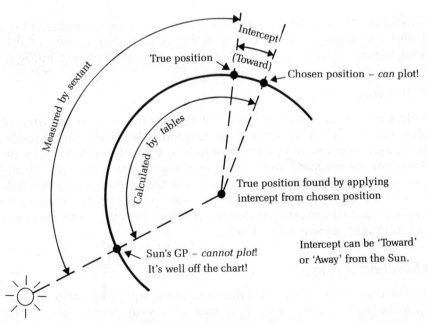

Fig 7   The principle of the PZX triangle solution.

azimuth runs through it, the intercept is stepped away from it, and the position line is drawn through it at right angles to the azimuth. When we compared the two altitudes, in this case true was *less* than tabulated, so the intercept moves *away* from the chosen position. (Note: GOAT – Greater Observed Altitude Towards.)

Now we can analyse the steps between the 'event points' in the chart.

Sextant Reading to True Altitude

You will see that there is a brief excursion into the Almanac to pick up some corrections. Fig 8 shows what the sextant does. The navigator sees the image of the Sun and measures its angle (altitude) above the horizon. Due to the Sun's enormous relative size, all rays strike the Earth at the same angle: they are parallel. Fig 8 shows that if you take the complement of the altitude (90° minus Alt.) you are in effect measuring the angular distance from the yacht to the geographical position of the body. This is called the *zenith distance* and can be converted to nautical miles over the Earth's surface by the exchange rate of 60 miles per degree. However, we leave it as altitude – as explained on page 15 (*see also* Fig 8).

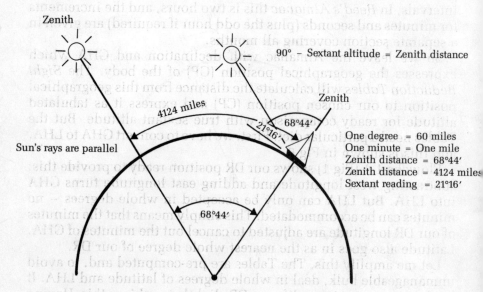

90° – Sextant altitude = Zenith distance

One degree = 60 miles
One minute = One mile
Zenith distance = 68°44′
Zenith distance = 4124 miles
Sextant reading = 21°16′

Fig 8   What the sextant does. Equivalence of angular and linear measurement.

It remains to explain the sextant corrections:

Index error   A small residual error, not practical to adjust out, checked by navigator before each shot.
Height of eye (dip)   Horizon falling away with height of eye above the sea.
Refraction   Bending of light rays by atmospheric refraction.
Semi-diameter   Correction from Sun's lower limb to centre.

These last three are basically what the Tables in the Almanac cover. This completes the charted path from observed sextant reading to true altitude.

Time (GMT) to Tabulated Altitude

Let us follow this path next. The flowchart (Fig 1) shows a route from the (GMT) time, through the Almanac and Tables, with the DR position lurking below to add its input. You will see that the Almanac accepts time and outputs declination and GHA. Having defined the body, the Sun in our case, time is expressed as: year-month-day-minute-second.

So, first ensure that you have the Almanac for the current year. There are blocks of data for each month, within which each day provides declination and Greenwich hour angle for specified time intervals. In *Reed's Almanac* this is two hours, and the increments for minutes and seconds (plus the odd hour if required) are given in a separate section covering all months.

So we leave the Almanac with declination and GHA which expresses the geographical position (GP) of the body. The *Sight Reduction Tables* will calculate the distance from this geographical position to our chosen position (CP) and express it as tabulated altitude for ready comparison with true sextant altitude. But the Tables need a particular diet. First, we have to convert GHA to LHA, and this is shown in Fig 9.

Flowchart A (Fig 1) shows our DR position ready to provide this: subtracting west longitude and adding east longitude turns GHA into LHA. But LHA can only be accepted in whole degrees – no minutes can be accommodated. This simply means that the minutes of our DR longitude are adjusted to cancel out the minutes of GHA. Latitude also goes in as the nearest whole degree of our DR.

Let me amplify this. The Tables are pre-computed and, to avoid unmanageable bulk, deal in whole degrees of latitude and LHA. It has been no sweat to modify our DR slightly to achieve this. Having done so, we can enter our chosen position on the chart. What

THE SUN SIGHT

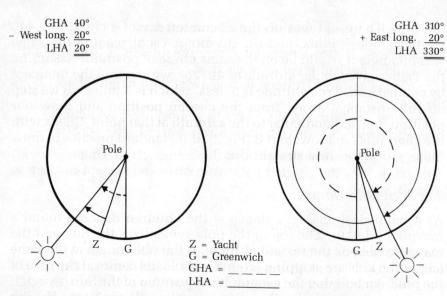

GHA 40°	GHA 310°
− West long. 20°	+ East long. 20°
LHA 20°	LHA 330°

Z = Yacht
G = Greenwich
GHA = _____
LHA = _____

Fig 9 Conversion of GHA (Greenwich hour angle) to LHA (local hour angle). This diagram shows that you subtract west long. and add east long. I suggest you simply apply this by rote, but the reasoning follows from the different treatments of terrestial longitude and hour angle. Terrestial longitude is stated east or west of Greenwich and cannot exceed 180°. Hour angle is stated westward up to the full 360°.

about declination? Well, we must include the minutes in the calculations but we do this by a separate loose sheet called 'Correction to Tabulated Altitude for Minutes of Declination'. (*See* Table 5, Fig 18.)

The Tables also output azimuth, the bearing of the body from the chosen position. So we can complete the plotting. We already have the chosen position, so we can draw in the azimuth, compare the two altitudes to obtain the intercept, and finally draw in the position line (PL).

The whole operation takes little time and is independent of power sources and external aids. This synopsis outlines the steps through flowchart A (Fig 1) on a 'need to know' basis, leaving analysis of the navigational figure until later. But we can take some representative figures to consolidate the picture. Assume the observed sextant angle was 49°08′, and we find the total correction is + 12′ giving 40°20′ true altitude. But stop for a moment to consider what it means. Its complement (90° minus 49°20′) is the zenith distance which is 40°40′ and this converts to 2,440 nautical miles. This is the actual distance of the yacht from the geographical position of the Sun. The yacht was on the circumference of a circle of 2,440 nautical miles radius, and on any other yacht reading the same sextant angle it would be on the same circle of position. Assuming the Tables give tabular altitude as 49°25′, we can find the intercept by comparison. True altitude is 5′ less, which is 5 miles, so we step off this distance 'away' from the chosen position and draw our position line perpendicular to the azimuth at that point. Check with the chart plots in Flowchart B (Fig 2). It is standard practice to draw the position line as a straight line.

The Maypole Dance

As a whimsical analogy, glance at the children dancing round a maypole (Fig 10). The top of the pole symbolizes the Sun and the maypole ribbons the sextant altitude. If the ribbons are at the same angle, the kids are skipping around a circle, its centre at the base of the pole symbolizing the geographical position of the Sun on top. If a child drifts inwards, the ribbon angle will increase: Greater Observed Angle Towards. Without straining the analogy too far, you can see that different distances from the centre can be related to intercepts.

Working the Flowcharts

We now need to 'flesh out' the Flowcharts, put numbers in and work through a few examples.

What goes in: DR position; observed sextant altitude; time (GMT).
What comes out: chosen position; azimuth; intercept; position line.
Working Publications: *Reed's Nautical Almanac* (1991):
3:37 GHA and declination for May 1991 (two-hour intervals) (Fig 12)
4:7 Increments for intermediate times (Fig 13)
4:5 Altitude Corrections – Sun's lower limb (Fig 14)
Sight Reduction Tables (Vol 3):
Pages 62–3 latitude 49° declination 15°/29° 'Same Name as latitude' (Figs 16 and 17)
Table 5 – Tabulated Altitude Correction for Minutes of Declination (Fig 18)

THE SUN SIGHT

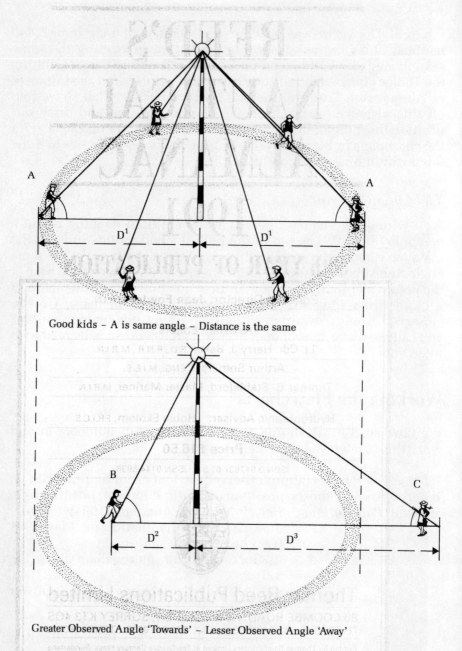

Good kids – A is same angle – Distance is the same

Greater Observed Angle 'Towards' – Lesser Observed Angle 'Away'

Fig 10   The Maypole Dance.

REED'S
NAUTICAL
ALMANAC
1991
60th YEAR OF PUBLICATION

Editorial Director: **Jean Fowler** M.R.I.N.

Assistant Editors:

Lt. Cdr. Harry J. Baker, R.D., R.N.R., M.R.I.N.

Arthur Somers, C.ENG., M.I.E.E.

Thomas B. Stableford, Master Mariner, M.R.I.N.

Hydrographic Adviser: Robin Ekblom, F.R.I.C.S.

Price £16.50

ISBN 0 947637 61 3   ISSN 0144-5936

Thomas Reed Publications Limited

80 COOMBE ROAD, NEW MALDEN, SURREY KT3 4QS
TELEPHONE: 081-949 7033/9   FAX: 081-949 0530   TELEX: 883526

Printed by Thomas Reed Printers Limited at The Double Century Press, Sunderland

Fig 11 Reed's Nautical Almanac *(1991), from which the extracts in this book are taken.*

Thursday, 16th May

G.M.T.	SUN G.H.A.	Dec.	ARIES G.H.A.	G.M.T.
00	180 55.4	N18 56.0	233 12.7	00
02	210 55.4	18 57.1	263 17.6	02
04	240 55.4	18 58.3	293 22.5	04
06	270 55.3	18 59.5	323 27.5	06
08	300 55.3	19 00.6	353 32.4	08
10	330 55.3	19 01.8	23 37.3	10
12	0 55.3	19 03.0	53 42.3	12
14	30 55.2	19 04.1	83 47.2	14
16	60 55.2	19 05.3	113 52.1	16
18	90 55.2	19 06.4	143 57.0	18
20	120 55.2	19 07.6	174 02.0	20
22	150 55.1	N19 08.7	204 06.9	22

Friday, 17th May

G.M.T.	SUN G.H.A.	Dec.	ARIES G.H.A.	G.M.T.
00	180 55.1	N19 09.9	234 11.8	00
02	210 55.1	19 11.0	264 16.7	02
04	240 55.1	19 12.2	294 21.7	04
06	270 55.0	19 13.3	324 26.6	06
08	300 55.0	19 14.4	354 31.5	08
10	330 55.0	19 15.6	24 36.5	10
12	0 54.9	19 16.7	54 41.4	12
14	30 54.9	19 17.8	84 46.3	14
16	60 54.9	19 19.0	114 51.2	16
18	90 54.8	19 20.1	144 56.2	18
20	120 54.8	19 21.2	175 01.1	20
22	150 54.7	N19 22.4	205 06.0	22

Saturday, 18th May

G.M.T.	SUN G.H.A.	Dec.	ARIES G.H.A.	G.M.T.
00	180 54.7	N19 23.5	235 11.0	00
02	210 54.7	19 24.6	265 15.9	02
04	240 54.6	19 25.7	295 20.8	04
06	270 54.6	19 26.8	325 25.7	06
08	300 54.5	19 27.9	355 30.7	08
10	330 54.5	19 29.0	25 35.6	10
12	0 54.4	19 30.1	55 40.5	12
14	30 54.4	19 31.3	85 45.5	14
16	60 54.4	19 32.4	115 50.4	16
18	90 54.3	19 33.5	145 55.3	18
20	120 54.3	19 34.5	176 00.2	20
22	150 54.2	N19 35.6	206 05.2	22

Sunday, 19th May

G.M.T.	SUN G.H.A.	Dec.	ARIES G.H.A.	G.M.T.
00	180 54.2	N19 36.7	236 10.1	00
02	210 54.1	19 37.8	266 15.0	02
04	240 54.0	19 38.9	296 20.0	04
06	270 54.0	19 40.0	326 24.9	06
08	300 53.9	19 41.1	356 29.8	08
10	330 53.9	19 42.2	26 34.7	10
12	0 53.8	19 43.2	56 39.7	12
14	30 53.8	19 44.3	86 44.6	14
16	60 53.7	19 45.4	116 49.5	16
18	90 53.7	19 46.5	146 54.5	18
20	120 53.6	19 47.5	176 59.4	20
22	150 53.5	N19 48.6	207 04.3	22

Monday, 20th May

G.M.T.	SUN G.H.A.	Dec.	ARIES G.H.A.	G.M.T.
00	180 53.5	N19 49.7	237 09.2	00
02	210 53.4	19 50.7	267 14.2	02
04	240 53.3	19 51.8	297 19.1	04
06	270 53.3	19 52.8	327 24.0	06
08	300 53.2	19 53.9	357 29.0	08
10	330 53.1	19 55.0	27 33.9	10
12	0 53.1	19 56.0	57 38.8	12
14	30 53.0	19 57.1	87 43.7	14
16	60 52.9	19 58.1	117 48.7	16
18	90 52.9	19 59.1	147 53.6	18
20	120 52.8	20 00.2	177 58.5	20
22	150 52.7	N20 01.2	208 03.4	22

Tuesday, 21st May

G.M.T.	SUN G.H.A.	Dec.	ARIES G.H.A.	G.M.T.
00	180 52.6	N20 02.3	238 08.4	00
02	210 52.6	20 03.3	268 13.3	02
04	240 52.5	20 04.3	298 18.2	04
06	270 52.4	20 05.4	328 23.2	06
08	300 52.3	20 06.4	358 28.1	08
10	330 52.3	20 07.4	28 33.0	10
12	0 52.2	20 08.4	58 37.9	12
14	30 52.1	20 09.5	88 42.9	14
16	60 52.0	20 10.5	118 47.8	16
18	90 51.9	20 11.5	148 52.7	18
20	120 51.9	20 12.5	178 57.7	20
22	150 51.8	N20 13.5	209 02.6	22

Wednesday, 22nd May

G.M.T.	SUN G.H.A.	Dec.	ARIES G.H.A.	G.M.T.
00	180 51.7	N20 14.5	239 07.5	00
02	210 51.6	20 15.5	269 12.4	02
04	240 51.5	20 16.5	299 17.4	04
06	270 51.4	20 17.5	329 22.3	06
08	300 51.4	20 18.5	359 27.2	08
10	330 51.3	20 19.5	29 32.2	10
12	0 51.2	20 20.5	59 37.1	12
14	30 51.1	20 21.5	89 42.0	14
16	60 51.0	20 22.5	119 46.9	16
18	90 50.9	20 23.5	149 51.9	18
20	120 50.8	20 24.5	179 56.8	20
22	150 50.7	N20 25.4	210 01.7	22

Thursday, 23rd May

G.M.T.	SUN G.H.A.	Dec.	ARIES G.H.A.	G.M.T.
00	180 50.6	N20 26.4	240 06.7	00
02	210 50.5	20 27.4	270 11.6	02
04	240 50.4	20 28.4	300 16.5	04
06	270 50.3	20 29.3	330 21.4	06
08	300 50.2	20 30.3	0 26.4	08
10	330 50.1	20 31.3	30 31.3	10
12	0 50.0	20 32.2	60 36.2	12
14	30 49.9	20 33.2	90 41.2	14
16	60 49.8	20 34.2	120 46.1	16
18	90 49.7	20 35.1	150 51.0	18
20	120 49.6	20 36.1	180 55.9	20
22	150 49.5	N20 37.0	211 00.9	22

Friday, 24th May

G.M.T.	SUN G.H.A.	Dec.	ARIES G.H.A.	G.M.T.
00	180 49.4	N20 38.0	241 05.8	00
02	210 49.3	20 38.9	271 10.7	02
04	240 49.2	20 39.9	301 15.6	04
06	270 49.1	20 40.8	331 20.6	06
08	300 49.0	20 41.8	1 25.5	08
10	330 48.9	20 42.7	31 30.4	10
12	0 48.8	20 43.6	61 35.4	12
14	30 48.7	20 44.5	91 40.3	14
16	60 48.5	20 45.5	121 45.2	16
18	90 48.4	20 46.4	151 50.1	18
20	120 48.3	20 47.3	181 55.1	20
22	150 48.2	N20 48.3	212 00.0	22

Saturday, 25th May

G.M.T.	SUN G.H.A.	Dec.	ARIES G.H.A.	G.M.T.
00	180 48.1	N20 49.2	242 04.9	00
02	210 48.0	20 50.1	272 09.9	02
04	240 47.9	20 51.0	302 14.8	04
06	270 47.7	20 51.9	332 19.7	06
08	300 47.6	20 52.8	2 24.6	08
10	330 47.5	20 53.7	32 29.6	10
12	0 47.4	20 54.6	62 34.5	12
14	30 47.3	20 55.5	92 39.4	14
16	60 47.1	20 56.4	122 44.4	16
18	90 47.0	20 57.3	152 49.3	18
20	120 46.9	20 58.2	182 54.2	20
22	150 46.8	N20 59.1	212 59.1	22

Sunday, 26th May

G.M.T.	SUN G.H.A.	Dec.	ARIES G.H.A.	G.M.T.
00	180 46.6	N21 00.0	243 04.1	00
02	210 46.5	21 00.9	273 09.0	02
04	240 46.4	21 01.8	303 13.9	04
06	270 46.3	21 02.7	333 18.9	06
08	300 46.1	21 03.5	3 23.8	08
10	330 46.0	21 04.4	33 28.7	10
12	0 45.9	21 05.3	63 33.6	12
14	30 45.7	21 06.2	93 38.6	14
16	60 45.6	21 07.0	123 43.5	16
18	90 45.5	21 07.9	153 48.4	18
20	120 45.3	21 08.8	183 53.4	20
22	150 45.2	N21 09.6	213 58.3	22

Monday, 27th May

G.M.T.	SUN G.H.A.	Dec.	ARIES G.H.A.	G.M.T.
00	180 45.1	N21 10.5	244 03.2	00
02	210 44.9	21 11.3	274 08.1	02
04	240 44.8	21 12.2	304 13.1	04
06	270 44.7	21 13.1	334 18.0	06
08	300 44.5	21 13.9	4 22.9	08
10	330 44.4	21 14.8	34 27.9	10
12	0 44.2	21 15.6	64 32.8	12
14	30 44.1	21 16.4	94 37.7	14
16	60 44.0	21 17.3	124 42.6	16
18	90 43.8	21 18.1	154 47.6	18
20	120 43.7	21 18.9	184 52.5	20
22	150 43.5	N21 19.8	214 57.4	22

Tuesday, 28th May

G.M.T.	SUN G.H.A.	Dec.	ARIES G.H.A.	G.M.T.
00	180 43.4	N21 20.6	245 02.3	00
02	210 43.2	21 21.4	275 07.3	02
04	240 43.1	21 22.3	305 12.2	04
06	270 42.9	21 23.1	335 17.1	06
08	300 42.8	21 23.9	5 22.1	08
10	330 42.6	21 24.7	35 27.0	10
12	0 42.5	21 25.5	65 31.9	12
14	30 42.3	21 26.3	95 36.8	14
16	60 42.2	21 27.1	125 41.8	16
18	90 42.0	21 27.9	155 46.7	18
20	120 41.9	21 28.7	185 51.6	20
22	150 41.7	N21 29.5	215 56.6	22

Wednesday, 29th May

G.M.T.	SUN G.H.A.	Dec.	ARIES G.H.A.	G.M.T.
00	180 41.6	N21 30.3	246 01.5	00
02	210 41.4	21 31.1	276 06.4	02
04	240 41.3	21 31.9	306 11.3	04
06	270 41.1	21 32.7	336 16.3	06
08	300 41.0	21 33.5	6 21.2	08
10	330 40.8	21 34.3	36 26.1	10
12	0 40.6	21 35.1	66 31.1	12
14	30 40.5	21 35.9	96 36.0	14
16	60 40.3	21 36.6	126 40.9	16
18	90 40.2	21 37.4	156 45.8	18
20	120 40.0	21 38.2	186 50.8	20
22	150 39.8	N21 39.0	216 55.7	22

Thursday, 30th May

G.M.T.	SUN G.H.A.	Dec.	ARIES G.H.A.	G.M.T.
00	180 39.7	N21 39.7	247 00.6	00
02	210 39.5	21 40.5	277 05.6	02
04	240 39.3	21 41.2	307 10.5	04
06	270 39.2	21 42.0	337 15.4	06
08	300 39.0	21 42.8	7 20.3	08
10	330 38.8	21 43.5	37 25.3	10
12	0 38.7	21 44.3	67 30.2	12
14	30 38.5	21 45.0	97 35.1	14
16	60 38.3	21 45.8	127 40.1	16
18	90 38.2	21 46.5	157 45.0	18
20	120 38.0	21 47.2	187 49.9	20
22	150 37.8	N21 48.0	217 54.8	224

Friday, 31st May

G.M.T.	SUN G.H.A.	Dec.	ARIES G.H.A.	G.M.T.
00	180 37.6	N21 48.7	247 59.8	00
02	210 37.5	21 49.4	278 04.7	02
04	240 37.3	21 50.2	308 09.6	04
06	270 37.1	N21 50.9	338 14.5	06
08	300 36.9	N21 51.6	8 19.5	08
10	330 36.8	21 52.3	38 24.4	10
12	0 36.6	21 53.1	68 29.3	12
14	30 36.4	N21 53.8	98 34.3	14
16	60 36.2	N21 54.5	128 39.2	16
18	90 36.0	21 55.2	158 44.1	18
20	120 35.9	21 55.9	188 49.0	20
22	150 35.7	N21 56.6	218 54.0	22

To interpolate SUN G.H.A. see page 4:7

To interpolate ARIES G.H.A. see page 4:8

Fig 12 Reed's Almanac *3:37*.

☉ SUN G.H.A. CORRECTION TABLE ☉

Min. or Sec.	Add for Minutes	Add for 1 Hour +Minutes	Add for Secs.		Min. or Sec.	Add for Minutes	Add for 1 Hour +Minutes	Add for Secs.
	° ′	° ′	′			° ′	° ′	′
0	0 0.0	15 0.0	0.0		30	7 30.0	22 30.0	7.5
1	0 15.0	15 15.0	0.3		31	7 45.0	22 45.0	7.8
2	0 30.0	15 30.0	0.5		32	8 0.0	23 0.0	8.0
3	0 45.0	15 45.0	0.8		33	8 15.0	23 15.0	8.3
4	1 0.0	16 0.0	1.0		34	8 30.0	23 30.0	8.5
5	1 15.0	16 15.0	1.3		35	8 45.0	23 45.0	8.8
6	1 30.0	16 30.0	1.5		36	9 0.0	24 0.0	9.0
7	1 45.0	16 45.0	1.8		37	9 15.0	24 15.0	9.3
8	2 0.0	17 0.0	2.0		38	9 30.0	24 30.0	9.5
9	2 15.0	17 15.0	2.3		39	9 45.0	24 45.0	9.8
10	2 30.0	17 30.0	2.5		40	10 0.0	25 0.0	10.0
11	2 45.0	17 45.0	2.8		41	10 15.0	25 15.0	10.3
12	3 0.0	18 0.0	3.0		42	10 30.0	25 30.0	10.5
13	3 15.0	18 15.0	3.3		43	10 45.0	25 45.0	10.8
14	3 30.0	18 30.0	3.5		44	11 0.0	26 0.0	11.0
15	3 45.0	18 45.0	3.8		45	11 15.0	26 15.0	11.3
16	4 0.0	19 0.0	4.0		46	11 30.0	26 30.0	11.5
17	4 15.0	19 15.0	4.3		47	11 45.0	26 45.0	11.8
18	4 30.0	19 30.0	4.5		48	12 0.0	27 0.0	12.0
19	4 45.0	19 45.0	4.8		49	12 15.0	27 15.0	12.3
20	5 0.0	20 0.0	5.0		50	12 30.0	27 30.0	12.5
21	5 15.0	20 15.0	5.3		51	12 45.0	27 45.0	12.8
22	5 30.0	20 30.0	5.5		52	13 0.0	28 0.0	13.0
23	5 45.0	20 45.0	5.8		53	13 15.0	28 15.0	13.3
24	6 0.0	21 0.0	6.0		54	13 30.0	28 30.0	13.5
25	6 15.0	21 15.0	6.3		55	13 45.0	28 45.0	13.8
26	6 30.0	21 30.0	6.5		56	14 0.0	29 0.0	14.0
27	6 45.0	21 45.0	6.8		57	14 15.0	29 15.0	14.3
28	7 0.0	22 0.0	7.0		58	14 30.0	29 30.0	14.5
29	7 15.0	22 15.0	7.3		59	14 45.0	29 45.0	14.8
					60	15 0.0	30 0.0	15.0

The above table is calculated on the assumption that the Sun changes her G.H.A. 15° in one hour, which it does on an average throughout the year. At certain times however, it may differ nearly 0.2 of a minute of arc from this. Little error will be occasioned for ordinary navigation if the lesser 2 hours is always worked from, when the above table will be additive.

Example of Use of above Table

(1) Required the Sun G.H.A. October 29th, 1991, at 9h. 27min. 38s. G.M.T.

October 29th 1991, G.M.T. 8h. (see p. 3:67) .... G.H.A. = 304° 03'.4

Correction from the above table for 1h. 27min. .... + = 21° 45'.0

      ″   ″   ″   ″   ″   ″ 38s. .... + = 9'.5

October 29th, 1991, at 9h. 27 min. 38s. .... G.H.A. = 325° 57'.9

Fig 13 Reed's Almanac *4:7*.

SUN ALTITUDE TOTAL CORRECTION TABLE
For correcting the Observed Altitude of the Sun's Lower Limb

ALWAYS ADDITIVE (+)
Height of the eye above the sea. Top line metres, lower line feet

| Obs. Alt. | 0.9 | 1.8 | 2.4 | 3 | 3.7 | 4.3 | 4.9 | 5.5 | 6 | 7.6 | 9 | 12 | 15 | 18 | 21 | 24 |
	3	6	8	10	12	14	16	18	20	25	30	40	50	60	70	80
9	8.6	8.0	7.6	7.2	6.9	6.6	6.4	6.2	5.9	5.4	4.9	4.1	3.4	2.7	2.1	1.5
10	9.1	8.5	8.1	7.9	7.5	7.2	7.0	6.7	6.6	6.0	5.5	4.7	3.9	3.3	2.7	2.1
11	9.6	9.0	8.6	8.3	8.0	7.7	7.4	7.2	7.0	6.4	6.0	5.2	4.4	3.7	3.1	2.5
12	10.0	9.4	9.0	8.7	8.4	8.1	7.8	7.6	7.4	6.8	6.4	5.6	4.8	4.1	3.5	2.9
13	10.3	9.7	9.3	9.0	8.7	8.4	8.2	7.9	7.7	7.2	6.7	5.9	5.2	4.5	3.9	3.3
14	10.6	10.0	9.6	9.3	9.0	8.7	8.5	8.2	8.0	7.5	7.0	6.2	5.5	4.8	4.2	3.6
15	10.9	10.2	9.9	9.5	9.2	9.0	8.7	8.5	8.2	7.7	7.2	6.4	5.7	5.0	4.4	3.8
16	11.1	10.5	10.1	9.7	9.5	9.2	8.9	8.7	8.5	7.9	7.5	6.7	5.9	5.2	4.6	4.1
17	11.3	10.7	10.3	10.0	9.7	9.4	9.1	8.9	8.7	8.2	7.7	6.9	6.1	5.5	4.9	4.3
18	11.5	10.8	10.5	10.1	9.9	9.6	9.3	9.1	8.9	8.3	7.9	7.0	6.3	5.6	5.0	4.5
19	11.6	11.0	10.6	10.3	10.0	9.7	9.5	9.2	9.0	8.5	8.0	7.2	6.5	5.8	5.2	4.6
20	11.8	11.2	10.8	10.4	10.2	9.9	9.6	9.4	9.2	8.6	8.2	7.4	6.6	5.9	5.3	4.8
21	11.9	11.3	10.9	10.6	10.3	10.0	9.8	9.5	9.3	8.8	8.3	7.5	6.8	6.1	5.5	4.9
22	12.0	11.4	11.0	10.7	10.4	10.1	9.9	9.7	9.4	8.9	8.4	7.6	6.9	6.2	5.6	5.0
23	12.1	11.5	11.1	10.8	10.5	10.2	10.0	9.8	9.5	9.0	8.5	7.7	7.0	6.3	5.7	5.1
24	12.2	11.6	11.2	10.9	10.6	10.3	10.1	9.9	9.6	9.1	8.6	7.8	7.1	6.4	5.8	5.2
25	12.3	11.7	11.3	11.0	10.7	10.4	10.2	10.0	9.7	9.2	8.7	7.9	7.2	6.5	5.9	5.3
26	12.4	11.8	11.4	11.1	10.8	10.5	10.3	10.1	9.8	9.3	8.8	8.0	7.3	6.6	6.0	5.4
27	12.5	11.9	11.5	11.2	10.9	10.6	10.4	10.1	9.9	9.4	8.9	8.1	7.4	6.7	6.1	5.5
28	12.6	12.0	11.6	11.3	11.0	10.7	10.4	10.2	10.0	9.5	9.0	8.2	7.4	6.8	6.2	5.6
30	12.7	12.1	11.7	11.4	11.1	10.8	10.6	10.4	10.1	9.6	9.1	8.3	7.6	6.9	6.3	5.7
32	12.9	12.2	11.9	11.5	11.2	11.0	10.7	10.5	10.2	9.7	9.3	8.4	7.7	7.0	6.4	5.8
34	13.0	12.3	12.0	11.6	11.3	11.1	10.8	10.6	10.3	9.8	9.4	8.5	7.8	7.1	6.5	5.9
36	13.1	12.4	12.1	11.7	11.4	11.2	10.9	10.7	10.4	9.9	9.5	8.6	7.9	7.2	6.6	6.0
38	13.2	12.5	12.1	11.8	11.5	11.2	11.0	10.8	10.5	10.0	9.5	8.7	8.0	7.3	6.7	6.1
40	13.3	12.6	12.2	11.9	11.6	11.3	11.1	10.8	10.6	10.1	9.6	8.8	8.1	7.4	6.8	6.2
42	13.4	12.7	12.3	12.0	11.7	11.4	11.2	10.9	10.7	10.2	9.7	8.9	8.2	7.5	6.9	6.3
44	13.4	12.7	12.4	12.0	11.7	11.5	11.2	11.0	10.7	10.2	9.8	8.9	8.2	7.5	6.9	6.3
46	13.5	12.8	12.4	12.1	11.8	11.5	11.3	11.0	10.8	10.3	9.8	9.0	8.3	7.6	7.0	6.4
48	13.6	12.9	12.5	12.2	11.9	11.6	11.3	11.1	10.9	10.4	9.9	9.1	8.3	7.7	7.1	6.4
50	13.6	12.9	12.5	12.2	11.9	11.6	11.4	11.1	10.9	10.4	9.9	9.1	8.4	7.7	7.1	6.5
52	13.6	13.0	12.6	12.3	12.0	11.7	11.4	11.2	11.0	10.5	10.0	9.2	8.4	7.8	7.2	6.5
54	13.7	13.0	12.6	12.3	12.0	11.7	11.5	11.3	11.0	10.5	10.0	9.2	8.5	7.8	7.2	6.6
56	13.7	13.1	12.7	12.4	12.1	11.8	11.5	11.3	11.1	10.6	10.1	9.3	8.5	7.9	7.3	6.7
58	13.8	13.1	12.7	12.4	12.1	11.8	11.6	11.3	11.1	10.6	10.1	9.3	8.6	7.9	7.3	6.8
60	13.8	13.1	12.8	12.4	12.1	11.9	11.6	11.4	11.1	10.6	10.2	9.3	8.6	7.9	7.3	6.8
62	13.9	13.2	12.8	12.5	12.2	11.9	11.7	11.4	11.2	10.7	10.2	9.4	8.7	8.0	7.4	6.8
64	13.9	13.2	12.8	12.5	12.2	11.9	11.7	11.5	11.2	10.7	10.2	9.4	8.7	8.0	7.4	6.9
66	14.0	13.2	12.9	12.5	12.3	12.0	11.7	11.5	11.3	10.7	10.3	9.5	8.7	8.1	7.5	7.0
70	14.1	13.3	12.9	12.6	12.3	12.0	11.8	11.6	11.3	10.8	10.3	9.5	8.8	8.1	7.5	7.0
80	14.2	13.5	13.1	12.8	12.5	12.2	11.9	11.7	11.5	11.0	10.5	9.7	8.9	8.3	7.7	7.1
90	14.3	13.6	13.2	12.9	12.6	12.3	12.1	11.9	11.6	11.1	10.6	9.8	9.1	8.4	7.8	7.2

MONTHLY CORRECTION

Jan.	Feb.	Mar.	Apr.	May	June	July	Aug.	Sept.	Oct.	Nov.	Dec.
+ 0'.3	+ 0'.2	+ 0'.1	0'.0	− 0'.1	− 0'.2	− 0'.2	− 0'.2	− 0'.1	+ 0'.1	+ 0'.2	+ 0'.3

Fig 14 Reed's Almanac *4:5.*

A.P. 3270

SIGHT REDUCTION TABLES
FOR
AIR NAVIGATION

VOLUME 3

LATITUDES 40°-89°
DECLINATIONS 0°-29°

Promulgated for the information and guidance of all concerned.

By Command of the Defence Council.

L.T.Durrett

LONDON: HER MAJESTY'S STATIONERY OFFICE

1967

Fig 15   Sight Reduction Tables for Air Navigation.

LHA	15° Hc	d	Z	16° Hc	d	Z	17° Hc	d	Z	18° Hc	d	Z	19° Hc	d	Z	20° Hc	d	Z	21° Hc	d	Z	22° Hc	d	Z
0	5600	+60	180	5700	+60	180	5800	+60	180	5900	+60	180	6000	+60	180	6100	+60	180	6200	+60	180	6300	+60	180
1	5559	60	178	5659	60	178	5759	60	178	5859	60	178	5959	60	178	6059	60	178	6159	60	178	6259	60	178
2	5558	60	177	5658	60	177	5758	60	176	5858	59	176	5957	60	176	6057	60	176	6157	60	176	6257	60	176
3	5555	60	175	5655	59	175	5754	60	175	5854	60	175	5954	60	174	6054	60	174	6154	60	174	6254	60	174
4	5551	59	173	5650	60	173	5750	60	173	5850	60	173	5950	59	173	6049	60	172	6149	60	172	6249	60	172
5	5545	+60	171	5645	+60	171	5745	+59	171	5844	+60	171	5944	+59	171	6043	+60	170	6143	+60	170	6243	+59	170
6	5539	60	170	5638	60	170	5738	59	169	5837	60	169	5937	59	169	6036	60	169	6136	59	168	6235	59	168
7	5531	60	168	5631	59	168	5730	59	168	5829	60	167	5929	59	167	6028	59	167	6127	59	166	6226	59	166
8	5522	60	166	5622	59	166	5721	59	166	5820	59	165	5919	59	165	6018	59	165	6117	59	164	6216	59	164
9	5513	59	165	5612	59	164	5711	58	164	5809	59	164	5908	59	163	6007	59	163	6106	58	162	6204	59	162
10	5502	+58	163	5600	+59	163	5659	+59	162	5758	+58	162	5856	+59	161	5955	+58	161	6053	+58	161	6151	+59	160
11	5450	58	161	5548	59	161	5647	58	161	5745	58	160	5843	58	160	5941	58	159	6039	58	159	6137	58	158
12	5436	59	160	5535	58	159	5633	58	159	5731	58	158	5829	58	158	5927	58	157	6025	57	157	6122	58	156
13	5422	58	158	5520	58	158	5618	58	157	5716	58	157	5814	57	156	5911	57	156	6008	58	155	6106	57	154
14	5407	58	157	5505	57	156	5602	58	156	5700	57	155	5757	57	155	5854	57	154	5951	57	153	6048	57	153
15	5351	+57	155	5448	+58	155	5546	+57	153	5643	+57	153	5740	+56	153	5836	+57	152	5933	+57	151	6030	+56	151
16	5334	57	153	5431	57	153	5528	57	152	5625	56	152	5721	57	151	5818	56	151	5914	56	150	6010	56	149
17	5316	57	152	5412	57	151	5509	56	151	5605	57	150	5702	56	150	5758	56	149	5854	55	148	5949	55	147
18	5257	56	150	5353	56	150	5449	56	149	5545	56	149	5641	56	148	5737	56	148	5832	55	146	5927	55	146
19	5237	56	149	5333	56	148	5429	55	148	5524	56	147	5620	55	146	5715	55	146	5810	55	145	5905	54	144
20	5216	+56	147	5312	+55	147	5407	+55	146	5502	+55	145	5557	+55	145	5652	+55	144	5747	+54	143	5841	+54	142
21	5154	55	146	5249	56	145	5345	55	145	5440	54	144	5534	55	143	5629	54	142	5723	54	142	5817	53	141
22	5132	55	144	5227	54	144	5321	55	143	5416	54	142	5510	54	142	5604	54	141	5658	53	140	5751	53	139
23	5108	55	143	5203	54	142	5257	54	142	5352	53	141	5445	54	140	5539	53	139	5632	53	139	5725	53	138
24	5044	55	142	5139	54	141	5233	53	140	5326	54	140	5420	53	139	5513	53	138	5606	52	137	5658	53	136
25	5019	+54	140	5113	+54	139	5207	+53	139	5300	+54	138	5354	+52	137	5446	+53	137	5539	+52	136	5631	+52	135
26	4954	54	139	5048	53	138	5141	54	138	5234	53	137	5327	52	136	5419	52	135	5511	52	134	5603	51	133
27	4928	53	138	5021	53	137	5114	52	136	5206	53	135	5259	52	135	5351	51	134	5442	52	133	5534	50	132
28	4901	53	136	4954	52	136	5046	52	135	5138	52	134	5230	52	133	5322	51	132	5413	51	131	5504	50	131
29	4833	53	135	4926	52	134	5018	52	134	5110	51	133	5201	52	132	5253	50	131	5343	51	130	5434	50	129
30	4805	+52	134	4857	+52	133	4949	+52	132	5041	+51	131	5132	+51	131	5223	+50	130	5313	+50	129	5403	+49	128
31	4736	52	133	4828	52	132	4920	51	131	5011	51	130	5102	50	129	5152	50	128	5242	50	128	5332	49	127
32	4707	51	131	4758	52	131	4850	50	130	4940	51	129	5031	50	128	5121	50	127	5211	49	126	5300	48	125
33	4637	51	130	4728	51	129	4819	50	128	4909	51	128	5000	49	127	5049	49	126	5138	49	125	5227	49	124
34	4607	51	129	4658	50	128	4748	50	127	4838	50	126	4928	49	126	5017	49	125	5106	48	124	5154	48	123
35	4536	+50	128	4626	+50	127	4716	+50	126	4806	+50	125	4856	+48	124	4944	+49	124	5033	+48	123	5121	+48	122
36	4504	50	127	4555	49	126	4644	50	125	4734	49	124	4823	48	123	4911	49	122	5000	47	121	5047	48	120
37	4433	49	125	4522	50	125	4612	49	124	4701	49	123	4750	48	122	4838	48	121	4926	47	120	5013	47	119
38	4400	50	124	4450	49	123	4539	49	122	4628	48	122	4716	48	121	4804	48	120	4852	47	119	4939	46	118
39	4327	50	123	4417	49	122	4506	49	122	4554	48	121	4642	48	120	4730	47	119	4817	47	118	4904	46	117
40	4254	+49	122	4343	+49	121	4432	+48	120	4520	+48	120	4608	+47	119	4655	47	118	4742	+47	117	4829	+46	116
41	4221	48	121	4309	49	120	4358	48	119	4446	47	119	4533	47	118	4620	47	117	4707	46	116	4753	46	115
42	4147	48	120	4235	48	119	4323	48	118	4411	47	118	4458	47	117	4545	46	115	4631	46	115	4717	46	114
43	4113	48	119	4201	47	118	4248	48	117	4336	47	116	4423	46	116	4509	46	115	4555	46	114	4641	45	113
44	4038	48	118	4126	47	117	4213	47	116	4300	47	115	4347	45	115	4433	46	114	4519	46	113	4605	45	112
45	4003	+47	117	4050	+48	116	4138	+47	115	4225	+46	114	4311	+46	114	4357	+46	113	4443	+45	112	4528	+45	111
46	3928	47	116	4015	47	115	4102	47	114	4149	46	113	4235	46	113	4321	45	112	4406	45	111	4451	45	110
47	3852	47	115	3939	47	114	4026	46	113	4112	46	112	4158	46	112	4244	45	111	4329	45	110	4414	44	109
48	3816	47	114	3903	47	113	3950	46	112	4036	46	111	4122	45	111	4207	45	110	4252	45	109	4337	44	108
49	3740	47	113	3827	46	112	3913	46	111	3959	46	111	4045	45	110	4130	45	109	4215	44	108	4259	44	107
50	3704	+46	112	3750	+46	111	3836	+46	110	3922	+45	110	4007	+44	109	4053	+44	108	4137	+44	107	4221	+44	106
51	3627	46	111	3713	46	110	3759	46	109	3845	45	109	3930	45	108	4015	44	107	4059	44	106	4143	44	105
52	3550	46	110	3636	46	109	3722	45	109	3807	46	108	3853	44	107	3937	44	106	4021	44	105	4105	44	104
53	3513	46	109	3559	46	108	3645	45	108	3730	45	107	3815	44	106	3859	44	105	3943	44	104	4027	43	103
54	3436	46	108	3522	45	108	3607	45	107	3652	45	106	3737	44	105	3821	44	104	3905	44	103	3949	43	102
55	3358	+46	107	3444	+45	107	3529	+45	106	3614	+45	105	3659	+44	104	3743	+44	103	3827	+43	103	3910	+43	102
56	3321	45	107	3406	45	106	3451	45	105	3536	44	104	3620	45	103	3705	43	103	3748	44	102	3832	43	101
57	3243	45	106	3328	45	105	3413	44	104	3458	44	103	3542	44	102	3626	44	102	3710	43	101	3753	43	100
58	3205	45	105	3250	45	104	3335	44	103	3419	44	102	3504	43	102	3547	44	101	3631	43	100	3714	43	99
59	3127	45	104	3212	45	103	3257	44	102	3341	44	102	3425	44	101	3509	43	100	3552	43	99	3635	43	98
60	3049	+44	103	3133	+45	102	3218	+44	102	3302	+44	101	3346	+44	100	3430	+43	99	3513	+43	98	3556	+43	97
61	3010	45	102	3055	44	102	3139	45	101	3224	43	100	3307	44	99	3351	43	98	3434	43	97	3517	43	97
62	2932	44	101	3016	45	101	3101	44	100	3145	44	99	3229	43	98	3312	43	98	3355	43	97	3438	42	96
63	2853	45	101	2938	44	100	3022	44	99	3106	44	98	3150	43	98	3233	43	97	3316	43	96	3359	42	95
64	2814	45	100	2859	44	99	2943	44	98	3027	44	98	3110	44	97	3154	43	96	3237	42	95	3319	43	94
65	2735	+45	99	2820	+44	99	2904	+44	98	2948	+43	97	3031	+44	96	3115	+43	95	3158	+42	94	3240	+43	93
66	2657	44	98	2741	44	97	2825	44	97	2909	44	96	2952	43	95	3035	43	94	3118	43	94	3201	42	93
67	2618	44	97	2702	44	97	2746	43	96	2829	44	95	2913	43	94	2956	43	94	3039	43	93	3122	42	92
68	2538	45	97	2623	44	96	2707	43	95	2750	44	94	2834	43	93	2917	43	92	3000	42	92	3042	42	91
69	2459	44	96	2543	44	95	2627	44	94	2711	43	94	2754	44	93	2837	43	92	2920	43	91	3003	42	90

Fig 16   Example 1.

28

23°			24°			25°			26°			27°			28°			29°			LHA
Hc	d	Z	Hc	d	Z	Hc	d	Z	Hc	d	Z	Hc	d	Z	Hc	d	Z	Hc	d	Z	
64 00	+60	180	65 00	+60	180	66 00	+60	180	67 00	+60	180	68 00	+60	180	69 00	+60	180	70 00	+60	180	360
63 59	60	178	64 59	60	178	65 59	60	178	66 59	60	178	67 59	60	178	68 59	60	178	69 59	59	177	359
63 57	60	176	64 57	60	176	65 57	60	176	66 57	60	175	67 57	60	175	68 57	60	175	69 57	59	175	358
63 54	59	174	64 53	60	174	65 53	60	173	66 53	60	173	67 53	59	173	68 52	60	173	69 52	60	172	357
63 49	59	172	64 48	60	171	65 48	59	171	66 47	60	171	67 47	60	171	68 47	59	170	69 46	60	170	356
63 42	+60	170	64 42	+59	169	65 41	+59	169	66 40	+60	169	67 40	+59	168	68 39	+59	168	69 38	+59	167	355
63 34	60	168	64 34	59	167	65 33	59	167	66 32	59	166	67 31	59	166	68 30	59	165	69 29	59	165	354
63 25	59	166	64 24	59	165	65 23	59	165	66 22	59	164	67 21	58	164	68 19	59	163	69 18	58	163	353
63 15	58	164	64 13	59	163	65 12	58	163	66 10	59	162	67 09	58	161	68 07	58	161	69 05	58	160	352
63 03	58	162	64 01	58	161	64 59	59	160	65 58	58	160	66 56	57	159	67 53	58	159	68 51	57	158	351
62 50	+58	160	63 48	+58	159	64 46	+57	158	65 43	+58	158	66 41	+57	157	67 38	+57	156	68 35	+57	155	350
62 35	58	158	63 33	57	157	64 30	58	156	65 28	57	156	66 25	57	155	67 22	56	154	68 18	57	153	349
62 20	57	156	63 17	57	155	64 14	57	154	65 11	56	154	66 07	57	153	67 04	56	152	68 00	55	151	348
62 03	57	154	63 00	56	153	63 56	57	152	64 53	56	152	65 49	56	151	66 45	55	150	67 40	55	149	347
61 45	56	152	62 41	56	151	63 37	56	150	64 33	56	150	65 29	55·	149	66 24	55	148	67 19	54	147	346
61 26	+56	150	62 22	+55	149	63 17	+55	148	64 13	+55	148	65 08	+55	147	66 03	+54	146	66 57	+54	145	345
61 06	55	148	62 01	55	148	62 56	55	147	63 51	55	146	64 46	54	145	65 40	53	144	66 34	53	143	344
60 44	55	147	61 39	54	146	62 34	55	145	63 29	54	144	64 23	53	143	65 16	53	142	66 09	53	141	343
60 22	55	145	61 17	54	144	62 11	54	143	63 05	54	142	63 58	54	141	64 51	53	140	65 44	52	139	342
59 59	54	143	60 53	54	142	61 47	53	141	62 40	53	140	63 33	53	139	64 26	51	138	65 17	52	137	341
59 35	+54	142	60 29	+53	140	61 22	+53	140	62 15	+52	139	63 07	+52	138	63 59	+51	137	64 50	+51	135	340
59 10	53	140	60 03	53	139	60 56	52	138	61 48	52	137	62 40	51	136	63 31	51	135	64 22	50	134	339
58 44	53	138	59 37	52	137	60 29	52	136	61 21	51	135	62 12	51	134	63 03	50	133	63 53	50	132	338
58 18	52	137	59 10	52	136	60 02	51	135	60 53	51	134	61 44	50	133	62 34	49	132	63 23	49	130	337
57 51	51	135	58 42	52	134	59 34	50	133	60 24	50	132	61 14	50	131	62 04	49	130	62 53	48	129	336
57 23	+51	134	58 14	+51	133	59 05	+50	132	59 55	+49	131	60 44	+50	130	61 34	+48	128	62 22	+48	127	335
56 54	51	132	57 45	50	131	58 35	50	130	59 25	49	129	60 14	48	128	61 02	48	127	61 50	48	126	334
56 24	51	131	57 15	50	130	58 05	49	129	58 54	49	128	59 43	48	127	60 31	47	126	61 18	47	124	333
55 54	50	129	56 44	50	127	57 34	48	128	58 22	49	126	59 11	47	125	59 58	47	124	60 45	46	123	332
55 24	49	128	56 13	49	127	57 02	48	126	57 50	48	125	58 38	47	124	59 25	47	123	60 12	46	121	331
54 52	+50	127	55 42	+48	126	56 30	+48	125	57 18	+47	124	58 05	+47	123	58 52	+46	121	59 38	+45	120	330
54 21	48	126	55 09	48	125	55 57	48	124	56 45	47	122	57 32	46	121	58 18	46	120	59 04	45	119	329
53 48	49	124	54 37	47	123	55 24	48	122	56 12	46	121	56 58	46	120	57 44	45	119	58 29	45	118	328
53 16	48	123	54 04	47	122	54 51	47	121	55 38	46	120	56 24	45	119	57 09	45	118	57 54	44	116	327
52 42	48	122	53 30	47	121	54 17	46	120	55 03	46	119	55 49	45	118	56 34	45	116	57 19	43	115	326
52 09	+47	121	52 56	+47	120	53 43	+46	119	54 29	+45	118	55 14	+45	116	55 59	+44	115	56 43	+43	114	325
51 35	47	119	52 22	46	118	53 08	45	117	53 53	46	116	54 39	44	115	55 23	44	114	56 07	43	113	324
51 00	47	118	51 47	46	117	52 33	46	116	53 18	45	115	54 03	44	114	54 47	43	113	55 30	43	112	323
50 25	47	117	51 12	45	116	51 57	45	115	52 42	44	113	53 27	43	113	54 10	43	112	54 53	43	111	322
49 50	46	116	50 36	45	115	51 21	45	114	52 06	44	113	52 50	44	111	53 34	42	111	54 16	43	110	321
49 15	+45	115	50 00	+45	114	50 45	+45	113	51 30	+44	112	52 14	+43	111	52 57	+42	110	53 39	+42	109	320
48 39	45	114	49 24	45	113	50 09	44	112	50 53	44	111	51 37	43	110	52 20	42	109	53 02	41	107	319
48 03	45	113	48 48	44	112	49 32	44	111	50 16	43	110	50 59	44	109	51 42	42	108	52 24	41	106	318
47 26	45	112	48 11	44	111	48 55	44	110	49 39	43	109	50 22	43	108	51 05	41	107	51 46	41	105	317
46 50	44	111	47 34	44	110	48 18	44	109	49 02	42	108	49 44	43	107	50 27	41	106	51 03	41	105	316
46 13	+44	110	46 57	+44	109	47 41	+43	108	48 24	+43	107	49 07	+42	106	49 49	+41	105	50 30	+41	104	315
45 36	44	109	46 20	43	108	47 03	43	107	47 46	43	106	48 29	42	105	49 11	41	104	49 52	40	103	314
44 58	44	108	45 42	44	107	46 26	42	106	47 08	43	105	47 51	41	104	48 32	41	103	49 13	41	102	313
44 21	43	107	45 04	44	106	45 48	42	105	46 30	42	104	47 12	42	103	47 54	41	102	48 35	40	101	312
43 43	43	106	44 26	43	105	45 09	43	104	45 52	41	104	46 34	41	102	47 15	41	101	47 56	40	100	311
43 05	+43	105	43 48	+43	104	44 31	+43	103	45 14	+41	102	45 55	+41	101	46 36	+41	100	47 17	+40	99	310
42 27	43	104	43 10	43	103	43 53	42	102	44 35	42	101	45 17	41	100	45 58	40	99	46 38	40	98	309
41 49	43	103	42 32	42	102	43 14	42	101	43 56	42	100	44 38	41	99	45 19	40	97	45 59	40	97	308
41 10	43	102	41 53	43	102	42 36	42	101	43 18	41	100	43 59	41	99	44 40	40	98	45 20	40	97	307
40 32	43	102	41 15	42	101	41 57	42	100	42 39	41	99	43 20	41	98	44 01	40	97	44 41	40	96	306
39 53	+43	101	40 36	+42	100	41 18	+42	99	42 00	+41	98	42 41	+41	97	43 22	+40	96	44 02	+39	95	305
39 15	42	100	39 57	42	99	40 39	42	98	41 21	41	97	42 02	41	96	42 42	40	95	43 22	40	94	304
38 36	42	99	39 18	42	98	40 00	42	97	40 42	41	96	41 23	40	95	42 03	40	93	42 43	40	93	303
37 57	42	98	38 39	42	97	39 21	41	96	40 02	41	95	40 43	41	94	41 24	40	93	42 04	39	92	302
37 18	42	97	38 00	42	96	38 42	41	96	39 23	41	95	40 04	41	94	40 45	40	93	41 25	39	92	301
36 39	+42	96	37 21	+42	96	38 03	+41	95	38 44	+41	94	39 25	+40	93	40 05	+40	92	40 45	+40	90	300
36 00	42	96	36 42	41	95	37 23	42	94	38 05	41	93	38 46	40	92	39 26	40	91	40 06	39	90	299
35 20	42	95	36 02	42	94	36 44	41	93	37 25	41	92	38 06	41	91	38 47	39	90	39 26	40	89	298
34 41	42	94	35 23	42	93	36 05	41	92	36 46	41	92	37 27	41	91	38 07	40	89	38 47	40	89	297
34 02	42	93	34 44	41	93	35 25	42	92	36 07	40	91	36 47	41	90	37 28	40	89	38 08	39	68	296
33 23	+41	93	34 04	+42	92	34 46	+41	91	35 27	+41	90	36 08	+40	89	36 48	+40	88	37 28	+40	87	295
32 43	42	92	33 25	42	91	34 07	41	90	34 48	41	89	35 29	40	88	36 09	40	87	36 49	40	86	294
32 04	42	91	32 46	41	90	33 27	42	89	34 09	40	88	34 49	41	88	35 30	40	87	36 10	39	86	293
31 24	42	90	32 06	42	89	32 48	41	89	33 29	41	88	34 10	41	87	34 51	40	86	35 31	39	85	292
30 45	42	90	31 27	42	89	32 09	41	88	32 50	41	87	33 31	40	86	34 11	40	85	34 51	40	84	291
23°			24°			25°			26°			27°			28°			29°			

NAME AS LATITUDE

LHA	15° Hc	d	Z	16° Hc	d	Z	17° Hc	d	Z	18° Hc	d	Z	19° Hc	d	Z	20° Hc	d	Z	21° Hc	d	Z	22° Hc	d	Z
70	2420	+44	95	2504	+44	94	2548	+44	94	2632	+43	93	2715	+43	92	2758	+43	91	2841	+43	90	2924	+42	90
71	2341	44	94	2425	44	94	2509	43	93	2552	44	92	2636	43	91	2719	43	90	2802	42	90	2844	42	89
72	2302	44	94	2346	43	93	2429	44	92	2513	43	91	2556	43	90	2639	43	90	2722	43	89	2805	42	88
73	2222	44	93	2306	44	92	2350	44	91	2434	43	90	2517	43	90	2600	43	89	2643	42	88	2725	43	87
74	2143	44	92	2227	44	91	2311	43	90	2354	44	90	2438	43	89	2521	43	88	2604	42	87	2646	42	87
75	2104	+44	91	2148	+43	90	2231	+44	90	2315	+43	89	2358	+43	88	2441	+43	87	2524	+43	87	2607	+42	86
76	2024	44	90	2108	44	90	2152	44	89	2236	43	88	2319	43	87	2402	43	87	2445	43	86	2528	42	85
77	1945	44	90	2029	44	89	2113	43	88	2156	44	87	2240	43	87	2323	43	86	2406	42	85	2448	43	84
78	1906	44	89	1950	43	88	2033	44	87	2117	43	87	2200	43	86	2244	43	85	2327	43	85	2409	43	84
79	1826	44	88	1910	44	87	1954	44	87	2038	43	86	2121	43	85	2204	43	85	2247	43	84	2330	43	83
80	1747	+44	87	1831	+44	87	1915	+44	86	1958	+44	85	2042	+43	85	2125	+43	84	2208	+43	83	2251	+43	82
81	1708	44	87	1752	43	86	1835	44	85	1919	44	85	2003	43	84	2046	43	83	2129	43	83	2212	43	82
82	1628	44	86	1712	44	85	1756	44	85	1840	44	84	1924	43	83	2007	43	82	2050	43	82	2133	43	81
83	1549	44	85	1633	44	84	1717	44	84	1801	44	83	1845	43	82	1928	43	82	2011	43	81	2054	43	80
84	1510	44	84	1554	44	84	1638	44	83	1722	44	82	1806	43	82	1849	44	81	1933	43	80	2016	43	79
85	1431	+44	84	1515	+44	83	1559	+44	82	1643	+44	82	1727	+43	81	1810	+44	80	1854	+43	79	1937	+43	79
86	1352	44	83	1436	44	82	1520	44	82	1604	44	81	1648	44	80	1732	43	79	1815	44	79	1859	43	78
87	1313	44	82	1357	44	82	1441	44	81	1525	44	80	1609	44	79	1653	44	79	1737	43	78	1820	43	77
88	1234	44	82	1318	44	81	1402	44	80	1446	44	79	1530	44	79	1614	44	78	1658	44	77	1742	43	77
89	1155	44	81	1239	45	80	1324	44	79	1408	44	79	1452	44	78	1536	44	77	1620	44	77	1704	43	76
90	1116	+44	80	1200	+45	79	1245	+44	79	1329	+44	78	1413	+45	77	1458	+44	77	1542	+43	76	1625	+44	75
91	1037	45	79	1122	44	79	1206	45	78	1251	44	77	1335	44	77	1419	44	76	1503	44	75	1547	44	74
92	0953	44	79	1043	45	78	1128	44	77	1212	45	77	1257	44	76	1341	45	75	1425	45	74	1510	44	74
93	0920	45	78	1005	45	77	1050	44	77	1134	45	76	1219	44	75	1303	45	74	1348	44	74	1432	44	73
94	0842	45	77	0927	44	76	1011	45	76	1056	45	75	1141	44	74	1225	45	74	1310	45	73	1354	45	72
95	0803	+45	76	0848	+45	76	0933	+45	75	1018	+45	74	1103	+45	74	1148	+44	73	1232	+45	72	1317	+44	72
96	0725	45	76	0810	45	75	0855	45	74	0940	45	74	1025	45	73	1110	45	72	1155	45	72	1240	44	71
97	0647	45	75	0732	45	74	0817	46	74	0903	45	73	0948	45	72	1033	45	72	1118	44	71	1202	45	70
98	0609	45	74	0654	45	74	0740	45	73	0825	45	72	0910	45	72	0955	45	71	1040	45	70	1125	45	70
99	0531	46	73	0617	45	73	0702	46	72	0748	45	72	0833	45	71	0918	45	70	1004	45	70	1049	45	69
100	0454	+45	73	0539	+46	72	0625	+45	71	0710	+46	71	0756	+45	70	0841	+46	69	0927	+45	69	1012	+45	68
101	0416	46	72	0502	46	71	0548	45	71	0633	46	70	0719	46	69	0805	45	69	0850	46	68	0936	46	67
102	0339	46	71	0425	46	70	0511	45	70	0556	46	69	0642	46	69	0728	46	68	0814	45	67	0859	46	67
103	0302	45	70	0348	46	70	0434	46	69	0520	46	69	0606	46	68	0652	46	67	0738	45	67	0823	46	66
104	0225	45	70	0311	46	69	0357	46	68	0443	46	68	0529	46	67	0615	47	67	0702	46	66	0748	45	65
105	0148	+46	69	0234	+46	68	0320	+47	68	0407	+46	67	0453	+46	66	0539	+47	66	0626	+46	65	0712	+46	65
106	0111	47	68	0158	46	68	0244	47	67	0331	46	66	0417	47	66	0504	46	65	0550	46	64	0636	47	64
107	0035	46	67	0121	47	67	0208	47	66	0255	46	66	0341	47	65	0428	47	64	0515	46	64	0601	47	63
108	-002	47	67	0045	47	66	0132	47	65	0219	47	65	0305	47	64	0353	46	64	0439	47	63	0526	47	62
109	-038	46	66	0009	47	65	0056	47	65	0143	47	64	0230	47	63	0317	47	63	0404	47	62	0451	47	62
110	-114	+48	65	-026	+47	65	0021	+47	64	0108	+47	63	0155	+48	63	0243	+47	62	0330	+47	62	0417	+47	61
111	-149	47	64	-102	48	64	-014	47	63	0033	47	63	0120	48	62	0208	47	61	0255	48	61	0343	47	60
112	-225	47	64	-137	48	63	-049	47	62	-002	48	62	0046	47	61	0133	48	61	0221	48	60	0309	47	59
113	-300	48	63	-212	48	62	-124	48	62	-036	47	61	0011	48	60	0059	48	60	0147	48	59	0235	48	59
114	-335	48	62	-247	48	62	-159	48	61	-111	48	60	-023	48	60	0025	48	59	0113	49	59	0201	48	58
115	-409	+48	61	-321	+48	61	-233	+48	60	-145	+48	60	-057	+49	59	-008	+48	58	0040	+48	58	0128	+48	57
116	-444	49	61	-355	48	60	-307	48	59	-219	49	59	-130	48	58	-042	49	58	0007	48	57	0055	49	56
117	-518	49	60	-429	48	59	-341	49	59	-252	49	58	-203	48	57	-115	49	57	-026	49	56	0023	48	55
118	-552	49	59	-503	49	58	-414	49	58	-325	48	57	-237	49	57	-148	49	56	-059	49	56	-010	49	55
119				-537	50	58	-447	49	57	-358	49	56	-309	49	55	-220	49	55	-131	49	55	-042	49	54
120							-520	+49	56	-431	+49	56	-342	+50	55	-252	+49	55	-203	+49	53	-114	+50	53
121							-553	50	55	-503	49	55	-414	50	54	-324	49	54	-235	50	53	-145	50	53
122										-536	50	54	-446	50	54	-356	50	53	-306	50	52	-216	50	52
123													-517	50	53	-427	50	52	-337	50	52	-247	51	51
124													-548	50	52	-458	50	51	-408	50	51	-318	51	50
125																-529	+51	51	-438	+50	50	-348	+51	50
126																-559	51	50	-508	51	49	-417	50	49
127																			-538	51	48	-447	51	48
128																						-516	51	47
129																						-545	52	46
130																								
131																								

15° 16° 17° 18° 19° 20° 21° 22°

Fig 17   Example 2.

NAME AS LATITUDE

23° Hc	d	Z	24° Hc	d	Z	25° Hc	d	Z	26° Hc	d	Z	27° Hc	d	Z	28° Hc	d	Z	29° Hc	d	Z	LHA
30 06	+42	89	30 19	+41	88	31 29	+42	87	32 11	+41	86	32 52	+41	85	33 32	+40	85	34 12	+41	84	290
29 25	42	88	30 08	42	87	30 50	41	86	31 31	41	86	32 12	41	85	32 53	40	84	33 33	40	83	289
28 47	42	87	29 29	42	87	30 11	41	86	30 52	41	85	31 33	41	84	32 14	40	83	32 54	40	82	288
28 08	42	87	28 50	42	86	29 32	42	85	30 13	41	84	30 54	41	83	31 35	40	82	32 15	40	82	287
27 28	43	86	28 11	41	85	28 52	42	84	29 34	41	83	30 15	41	83	30 56	40	82	31 35	40	81	286
26 49	+42	85	27 31	+42	84	28 13	+42	84	28 55	+41	83	29 36	+41	82	30 17	+41	81	30 57	+41	80	285
26 10	42	84	26 52	42	84	27 34	42	83	28 16	41	82	28 57	41	81	29 38	41	80	30 19	40	79	284
25 31	42	84	26 13	42	83	26 55	42	82	27 37	41	81	28 18	41	80	28 59	41	80	29 40	41	79	283
24 52	42	83	25 34	42	82	26 16	42	81	26 58	41	81	27 39	42	80	28 21	41	79	29 02	40	78	282
24 13	42	82	24 55	42	81	25 37	42	81	26 19	42	80	27 01	41	79	27 42	41	78	28 23	41	77	281
23 34	42	82	24 16	+42	81	24 58	+42	80	25 40	+42	79	26 22	+42	78	27 04	+41	78	27 45	+41	77	280
22 55	42	81	23 37	43	80	24 20	42	79	25 02	42	78	25 44	41	78	26 25	41	77	27 06	42	76	279
22 16	43	80	22 59	42	79	23 41	42	79	24 23	42	78	25 05	42	77	25 47	41	76	26 28	41	75	278
21 37	43	79	22 20	43	79	23 03	42	78	23 45	42	77	24 27	42	76	25 09	41	76	25 50	42	75	277
20 59	43	79	21 42	42	78	22 24	43	77	23 07	42	76	23 49	42	76	24 31	41	75	25 12	42	74	276
20 20	+43	78	21 03	+43	77	21 46	+42	76	22 28	+43	75	23 11	+42	75	23 53	+42	74	24 35	+41	73	275
19 42	44	77	20 25	43	77	21 08	42	76	21 50	43	75	22 33	42	74	23 15	42	73	23 57	42	73	274
19 03	44	77	19 47	43	76	20 30	42	75	21 12	43	74	21 55	42	74	22 37	42	73	23 19	42	72	273
18 25	43	76	19 08	44	75	19 52	43	75	20 35	42	74	21 17	43	73	22 00	42	72	22 42	42	71	272
17 47	43	75	18 30	44	74	19 14	43	74	19 57	43	73	20 40	43	72	21 22	43	71	22 05	42	71	271
17 09	+44	74	17 53	+43	74	18 36	+43	73	19 19	+43	72	20 02	+43	72	20 45	+43	71	21 28	+42	70	270
16 31	44	74	17 15	43	73	17 58	44	72	18 42	43	72	19 25	43	71	20 08	43	70	20 51	43	69	269
15 54	43	73	16 37	44	72	17 21	44	72	18 05	43	71	18 48	43	70	19 31	43	69	20 14	43	69	268
15 16	44	72	16 00	44	72	16 44	43	71	17 27	44	70	18 11	43	70	18 54	44	69	19 38	43	68	267
14 39	44	72	15 23	44	71	16 07	44	70	16 50	44	70	17 34	44	69	18 18	43	68	19 01	43	68	266
14 01	+45	71	14 46	+44	70	15 30	+44	70	16 14	+44	69	16 58	+43	68	17 41	+44	67	18 25	+43	67	265
13 24	45	70	14 09	44	70	14 53	44	69	15 37	44	68	16 21	44	67	17 05	44	67	17 49	43	66	264
12 47	45	70	13 32	44	69	14 16	45	68	15 01	44	68	15 45	44	67	16 29	44	66	17 13	44	65	263
12 10	45	69	12 55	45	68	13 40	44	68	14 24	45	67	15 09	44	66	15 53	44	65	16 37	44	65	262
11 34	45	68	12 19	45	67	13 04	44	67	13 43	45	66	14 33	44	65	15 17	45	65	16 02	44	64	261
10 57	+45	67	11 42	+45	67	12 27	+45	66	13 12	+45	65	13 57	+45	65	14 42	+45	64	15 27	+44	63	260
10 21	45	67	11 06	46	66	11 52	45	65	12 37	45	65	13 22	45	64	14 07	44	63	14 51	45	63	259
09 45	46	66	10 30	45	65	11 16	45	65	12 01	45	64	12 46	46	63	13 32	45	63	14 17	45	62	258
09 09	46	65	09 55	45	65	10 40	45	64	11 26	45	63	12 11	46	62	12 57	45	62	13 42	45	61	257
08 33	46	65	09 19	46	64	10 05	46	63	10 51	46	63	11 37	45	62	12 22	46	61	13 08	45	61	256
07 58	+46	64	08 44	+46	63	09 30	+46	62	10 16	+46	62	11 02	+46	61	11 48	+45	61	12 33	+46	60	255
07 23	46	63	08 09	46	63	08 55	46	62	09 41	47	61	10 28	45	61	11 13	46	60	11 59	46	59	254
06 48	46	62	07 34	47	62	08 21	46	61	09 07	46	60	09 53	47	60	10 40	46	59	11 26	46	59	253
06 13	47	62	07 00	46	61	07 46	47	61	08 33	46	60	09 19	47	59	10 06	46	59	10 52	47	58	252
05 33	47	61	06 25	47	60	07 12	47	60	07 59	47	60	08 46	46	59	09 32	47	58	10 19	47	57	251
05 04	+47	60	05 51	+47	60	06 38	+47	59	07 25	+47	59	08 12	+47	58	08 59	+47	57	09 46	+47	57	250
04 30	47	60	05 17	48	59	06 05	47	58	06 52	47	58	07 39	47	57	08 26	47	56	09 13	47	56	249
03 56	49	59	04 44	47	58	05 31	48	58	06 19	47	57	07 06	48	56	07 54	47	56	08 41	47	55	248
03 23	47	58	04 10	48	57	04 58	48	57	05 46	48	56	06 34	47	56	07 21	48	55	08 09	47	54	247
02 49	47	57	03 37	48	57	04 25	48	56	05 13	48	56	06 01	48	55	06 49	48	54	07 37	48	54	246
02 16	+49	57	03 05	+48	56	03 53	+48	55	04 41	+48	55	05 29	+48	54	06 17	+48	54	07 05	+48	53	245
01 44	48	56	02 32	47	55	03 21	48	55	04 09	48	54	04 57	49	54	05 46	48	53	06 34	48	52	244
01 11	47	55	02 00	49	55	02 49	48	54	03 37	49	53	04 26	48	53	05 14	49	52	06 03	49	52	243
00 39	48	54	01 28	49	54	02 17	49	54	03 06	49	53	03 55	49	52	04 43	49	51	05 32	49	51	242
00 07	49	54	00 56	50	53	01 46	49	52	02 35	49	52	03 24	49	51	04 13	49	51	05 02	49	50	241
−0 24	+49	53	00 25	+49	52	01 14	+50	52	02 04	+49	51	02 53	+50	51	03 43	+49	50	04 32	+49	49	240
−0 56	50	52	−0 06	50	52	00 44	49	51	01 33	50	50	02 23	50	50	03 13	49	49	04 02	50	49	239
−1 26	49	51	−0 37	50	51	00 13	50	50	01 03	50	50	01 53	50	49	02 43	50	49	03 33	50	48	238
−1 57	50	51	−1 07	50	50	−0 17	50	49	00 33	50	49	01 23	51	48	02 14	50	48	03 04	50	47	237
−2 27	50	50	−1 37	51	49	−0 46	50	49	00 04	50	48	00 54	51	48	01 45	50	47	02 35	50	47	236
−2 57	+50	49	−2 07	+51	48	−1 16	+51	48	−0 25	+50	47	00 25	+51	47	01 16	+50	46	02 06	+51	46	235
−3 27	51	48	−2 36	51	48	−1 45	51	47	−0 54	51	47	−0 03	51	46	00 48	50	45	01 38	51	45	234
−3 56	51	47	−3 05	51	47	−2 14	51	46	−1 23	52	46	−0 31	51	45	00 20	51	45	01 11	51	44	233
−4 25	52	47	−3 33	51	46	−2 42	51	46	−1 51	52	45	−0 59	51	45	−0 08	51	44	00 43	51	44	232
−4 53	51	46	−4 02	52	45	−3 10	51	45	−2 18	51	44	−1 27	52	44	−0 35	51	43	00 16	52	43	231
−5 21	+52	45	−4 29	+51	45	−3 38	+52	44	−2 46	+52	44	−1 54	+52	43	−1 02	+52	43	−0 10	+52	42	230
−5 49	52	44	−4 57	52	44	−4 05	52	43	−3 13	52	43	−2 21	52	42	−1 28	52	42	−0 35	52	41	229
		132	−5 24	53	43	−4 32	53	42	−3 39	52	42	−2 47	52	42	−1 54	52	41	−1 02	52	41	228
		133	−5 51	53	42	−4 58	53	42	−4 05	52	41	−3 13	53	41	−2 20	53	40	−1 27	52	40	227
					134	−5 24	53	41	−4 31	53	40	−3 38	53	40	−2 45	53	39	−1 52	53	39	226
					135	−5 50	+54	40	−4 56	+53	40				−3 10	+53	39	−2 17	+53	38	225
								136	−5 21	53	39	−4 28	53	38				−2 41	53	37	224
								137	−5 46	54	38	−4 52	53	38				−3 05	53	37	223
											138	−5 16	54	37	−4 22	54	36				222
											139	−5 39	54	36	−4 45	54	35				221

23°	24°	25°	26°	27°	28°	29°

NAME AS LATITUDE

LAT 49°

TABLE 5.—Correction to Tabulated

d/	1	2	3	4	5	6	7	8	9	10	11	12	13	14	15	16	17	18	19	20	21	22	23	24	25	26	27	28	29	30
0	0	0	0	0	0	0	0	0	0	0	0	0	0	0	0	0	0	0	0	0	0	0	0	0	0	0	0	0	0	0
1	0	0	0	0	0	0	0	0	0	0	0	0	0	0	0	0	0	0	0	0	0	0	0	0	0	0	0	0	0	0
2	0	0	0	0	0	0	0	0	0	0	0	0	0	0	0	1	1	1	1	1	1	1	1	1	1	1	1	1	1	1
3	0	0	0	0	0	0	0	0	0	0	1	1	1	1	1	1	1	1	1	1	1	1	1	1	1	1	1	1	1	1
4	0	0	0	0	0	0	0	1	1	1	1	1	1	1	1	1	1	1	1	1	1	1	2	2	2	2	2	2	2	2
5	0	0	0	0	0	0	1	1	1	1	1	1	1	1	1	1	1	2	2	2	2	2	2	2	2	2	2	2	2	2
6	0	0	0	0	0	1	1	1	1	1	1	1	1	1	2	2	2	2	2	2	2	2	2	2	2	3	3	3	3	3
7	0	0	0	0	1	1	1	1	1	1	1	1	2	2	2	2	2	2	2	2	2	3	3	3	3	3	3	3	3	4
8	0	0	0	1	1	1	1	1	1	1	1	2	2	2	2	2	2	2	3	3	3	3	3	3	3	3	4	4	4	4
9	0	0	0	1	1	1	1	1	1	2	2	2	2	2	2	2	3	3	3	3	3	3	3	4	4	4	4	4	4	4
10	0	0	0	1	1	1	1	1	2	2	2	2	2	2	2	3	3	3	3	3	4	4	4	4	4	4	4	5	5	5
11	0	0	1	1	1	1	1	1	2	2	2	2	2	3	3	3	3	3	3	4	4	4	4	4	5	5	5	5	5	6
12	0	0	1	1	1	1	1	2	2	2	2	2	3	3	3	3	3	4	4	4	4	4	5	5	5	5	5	6	6	6
13	0	0	1	1	1	1	2	2	2	2	2	3	3	3	3	3	4	4	4	4	5	5	5	5	5	6	6	6	6	6
14	0	0	1	1	1	1	2	2	2	2	3	3	3	3	3	4	4	4	4	5	5	5	5	6	6	6	6	7	7	7
15	0	0	1	1	1	2	2	2	3	2	3	3	3	4	4	4	4	4	5	5	5	6	6	6	6	6	7	7	7	8
16	0	1	1	1	1	2	2	2	2	3	3	3	3	4	4	4	5	5	5	5	6	6	6	6	7	7	7	7	8	8
17	0	1	1	1	1	2	2	2	3	3	3	3	4	4	4	5	5	5	5	6	6	6	7	7	7	7	8	8	8	8
18	0	1	1	1	2	2	2	2	3	3	3	4	4	4	4	5	5	5	6	6	6	7	7	7	8	8	8	8	9	9
19	0	1	1	1	2	2	2	3	3	3	3	4	4	4	5	5	5	6	6	6	7	7	7	8	8	8	9	9	9	10
20	0	1	1	1	2	2	2	3	3	3	4	4	4	5	5	5	6	6	6	7	7	7	8	8	8	9	9	9	10	10
21	0	1	1	1	2	2	2	3	3	4	4	4	5	5	5	6	6	6	7	7	7	8	8	8	9	9	9	10	10	10
22	0	1	1	1	2	2	3	3	3	4	4	4	5	5	6	6	6	7	7	7	8	8	8	9	9	10	10	10	11	11
23	0	1	1	2	2	2	3	3	3	4	4	5	5	5	6	6	7	7	7	8	8	8	9	9	10	10	10	11	11	11
24	0	1	1	2	2	2	3	3	4	4	4	5	5	6	6	6	7	7	8	8	8	9	9	10	10	10	11	11	12	12
25	0	1	1	2	2	2	3	3	4	4	5	5	5	6	6	7	7	8	8	8	9	9	10	10	10	11	11	12	12	12
26	0	1	1	2	2	3	3	3	4	4	5	5	6	6	6	7	7	8	8	9	9	10	10	10	11	11	12	12	13	13
27	0	1	1	2	2	3	3	4	4	4	5	5	6	6	7	7	8	8	9	9	9	10	10	11	11	12	12	13	13	14
28	0	1	1	2	2	3	3	4	4	5	5	6	6	7	7	7	8	8	9	9	10	10	11	11	12	12	13	13	14	14
29	0	1	1	2	2	3	3	4	4	5	5	6	6	7	7	8	8	9	9	10	10	11	11	12	12	13	13	14	14	14
30	0	1	2	2	2	3	4	4	4	5	6	6	6	7	8	8	8	9	10	10	10	11	12	12	12	13	14	14	14	15
31	1	1	2	2	3	3	4	4	5	5	6	6	7	7	8	8	9	9	10	10	11	11	12	12	13	13	14	14	15	16
32	1	1	2	2	3	3	4	4	5	5	6	6	7	7	8	9	9	10	10	11	11	12	12	13	13	14	14	15	15	16
33	1	1	2	2	3	3	4	4	5	6	6	7	7	8	8	9	9	10	10	11	12	12	13	13	14	14	15	15	16	16
34	1	1	2	2	3	3	4	5	5	6	6	7	7	8	8	9	10	10	11	11	12	12	13	14	14	15	15	16	16	17
35	1	1	2	2	3	4	4	5	5	6	6	7	8	8	9	9	10	10	11	12	12	13	13	14	15	15	16	16	17	18
36	1	1	2	2	3	4	4	5	5	6	7	7	8	8	9	10	10	11	11	12	13	13	14	14	15	16	16	17	17	18
37	1	1	2	2	3	4	4	5	6	6	7	7	8	9	9	10	10	11	12	12	13	14	14	15	15	16	17	17	18	18
38	1	1	2	3	3	4	4	5	6	6	7	8	8	9	10	10	11	11	12	13	13	14	15	15	16	16	17	18	18	19
39	1	1	2	3	3	4	5	5	6	6	7	8	8	9	10	10	11	12	12	13	14	14	15	16	16	17	18	18	19	20
40	1	1	2	3	3	4	5	5	6	7	7	8	9	9	10	11	11	12	13	13	14	15	15	16	17	17	18	19	19	20
41	1	1	2	3	3	4	5	5	6	7	8	8	9	10	10	11	12	12	13	14	14	15	16	16	17	18	18	19	20	20
42	1	1	2	3	4	4	5	6	6	7	8	8	9	10	10	11	12	13	13	14	15	15	16	17	18	18	19	20	20	21
43	1	1	2	3	4	4	5	6	6	7	8	9	9	10	11	11	12	13	14	14	15	16	16	17	18	19	19	20	21	22
44	1	1	2	3	4	4	5	6	7	7	8	9	10	10	11	12	12	13	14	15	15	16	17	18	18	19	20	21	21	22
45	1	2	2	3	4	4	5	6	7	8	8	9	10	10	11	12	13	14	14	15	16	16	17	18	19	20	20	21	22	22
46	1	2	2	3	4	5	5	6	7	8	8	9	10	11	12	12	13	14	15	15	16	17	18	18	19	20	21	21	22	23
47	1	2	2	3	4	5	5	6	7	8	9	9	10	11	12	13	13	14	15	16	16	17	18	19	20	20	21	22	23	24
48	1	2	2	3	4	5	6	6	7	8	9	10	10	11	12	13	14	14	15	16	17	18	18	19	20	21	22	22	23	24
49	1	2	2	3	4	5	6	7	7	8	9	10	11	11	12	13	14	15	16	16	17	18	19	20	20	21	22	23	24	24
50	1	2	2	3	4	5	6	7	8	8	9	10	11	12	12	13	14	15	16	17	18	18	19	20	21	22	22	23	24	25
51	1	2	3	3	4	5	6	7	8	8	9	10	11	12	13	14	14	15	16	17	18	19	20	20	21	22	23	24	25	26
52	1	2	3	3	4	5	6	7	8	9	10	10	11	12	13	14	15	16	16	17	18	19	20	21	22	23	23	24	25	26
53	1	2	3	4	4	5	6	7	8	9	10	11	11	12	13	14	15	16	17	18	19	19	20	21	22	23	24	25	26	26
54	1	2	3	4	4	5	6	7	8	9	10	11	12	13	14	14	15	17	17	18	19	20	21	22	22	23	24	25	26	27
55	1	2	3	4	5	6	6	7	8	9	10	11	12	13	14	15	15	16	17	18	19	20	21	22	23	24	25	26	27	28
56	1	2	3	4	5	6	7	7	8	9	10	11	12	13	14	15	15	17	18	19	20	21	21	22	23	24	25	26	27	28
57	1	2	3	4	5	6	7	8	9	10	10	11	12	13	14	15	16	17	18	19	20	21	22	23	24	25	26	27	28	28
58	1	2	3	4	5	6	7	8	9	10	11	12	13	14	14	15	16	17	18	19	20	21	22	23	24	25	26	27	28	29
59	1	2	3	4	5	6	7	8	9	10	11	12	13	14	15	16	17	18	19	20	21	22	23	24	25	26	27	28	29	30

Fig 18   Table 5 – Correction to Tabulated Altitude for Minutes of Declination.

Altitude for Minutes of Declination

31 32 33	34 35 36	37 38 39	40 41 42	43 44 45	46 47 48	49 50 51	52 53 54	55 56 57	58 59 60	d / ′
0 0 0	0 0 0	0 0 0	0 0 0	0 0 0	0 0 0	0 0 0	0 0 0	0 0 0	0 0 0	0
1 1 1	1 1 1	1 1 1	1 1 1	1 1 1	1 1 1	1 1 1	1 1 1	1 1 1	1 1 1	1
1 1 1	1 1 1	1 1 1	1 1 1	1 1 2	2 2 2	2 2 2	2 2 2	2 2 2	2 2 2	2
2 2 2	2 2 2	2 2 2	2 2 2	2 2 2	2 2 2	2 2 3	3 3 3	3 3 3	3 3 3	3
2 2 2	2 2 2	2 3 3	3 3 3	3 3 3	3 3 3	3 3 3	3 4 4	4 4 4	4 4 4	4
3 3 3	3 3 3	3 3 3	3 3 4	4 4 4	4 4 4	4 4 4	4 4 4	5 5 5	5 5 5	5
3 3 3	3 4 4	4 4 4	4 4 4	4 4 4	5 5 5	5 5 5	5 5 5	6 6 6	6 6 6	6
4 4 4	4 4 4	4 4 5	5 5 5	5 5 5	5 5 6	6 6 6	6 6 6	6 7 7	7 7 7	7
4 4 4	5 5 5	5 5 5	5 5 6	6 6 6	6 6 6	7 7 7	7 7 7	7 7 8	8 8 8	8
5 5 5	5 5 5	6 6 6	6 6 6	6 7 7	7 7 7	7 8 8	8 8 8	8 8 9	9 9 9	9
5 5 6	6 6 6	6 6 6	7 7 7	7 7 8	8 8 8	8 8 8	9 9 9	9 9 10	10 10 10	10
6 6 6	6 6 7	7 7 7	7 8 8	8 8 8	8 9 9	9 9 9	10 10 10	10 10 10	11 11 11	11
6 6 7	7 7 7	7 8 8	8 8 8	9 9 9	9 9 10	10 10 10	10 11 11	11 11 11	12 12 12	12
7 7 7	7 8 8	8 8 8	9 9 9	9 10 10	10 10 10	11 11 11	11 11 12	12 12 12	13 13 13	13
7 7 8	8 8 8	9 9 9	9 10 10	10 10 10	11 11 11	11 12 12	12 12 13	13 13 13	14 14 14	14
8 8 8	8 9 9	9 10 10	10 10 10	11 11 11	12 12 12	12 12 13	13 13 14	14 14 14	14 15 15	15
8 9 9	9 9 10	10 10 10	11 11 11	11 12 12	12 13 13	13 13 14	14 14 14	15 15 15	15 16 16	16
9 9 9	10 10 10	10 11 11	11 12 12	12 12 13	13 13 14	14 14 14	15 15 15	16 16 16	16 17 17	17
9 10 10	10 10 11	11 11 12	12 12 13	13 13 14	14 14 14	15 15 15	16 16 16	16 17 17	17 18 18	18
10 10 10	11 11 11	12 12 12	13 13 13	14 14 14	15 15 15	16 16 16	16 17 17	17 18 18	18 19 19	19
10 11 11	11 12 12	12 13 13	13 14 14	14 15 15	15 16 16	16 17 17	17 18 18	18 19 19	19 20 20	20
11 11 12	12 12 13	13 13 14	14 14 15	15 15 16	16 16 17	17 18 18	18 19 19	19 20 20	20 21 21	21
11 12 12	12 13 13	14 14 14	15 15 15	16 16 16	17 17 18	18 18 19	19 19 20	20 21 21	21 22 22	22
12 12 13	13 13 14	14 15 15	15 16 16	16 17 17	18 18 18	19 19 20	20 20 21	21 21 22	22 23 23	23
12 13 13	14 14 14	15 15 16	16 16 17	17 18 18	18 19 19	20 20 20	21 21 22	22 22 23	23 24 24	24
13 13 14	14 15 15	15 16 16	17 17 18	18 18 19	19 20 20	20 21 21	22 22 22	23 23 24	24 25 25	25
13 14 14	15 15 16	16 16 17	17 18 18	19 19 20	20 20 21	21 22 22	23 23 23	24 24 25	25 26 26	26
14 14 15	15 16 16	17 17 18	18 18 19	19 20 20	21 21 22	22 22 23	23 24 24	25 25 26	26 27 27	27
14 15 15	16 16 17	17 18 18	19 19 20	20 21 21	21 22 22	23 23 24	24 25 25	26 26 27	27 28 28	28
15 15 16	16 17 17	18 18 19	19 20 20	21 21 22	22 23 23	24 24 25	25 26 26	27 27 28	28 29 29	29
16 16 16	17 18 18	18 19 20	20 20 21	22 22 22	23 24 24	24 25 26	26 26 27	28 28 28	29 30 30	30
16 17 17	18 18 19	19 20 20	21 21 22	22 23 23	24 24 25	25 26 26	27 27 28	28 29 29	30 30 31	31
17 17 18	18 19 19	20 20 21	21 22 22	23 23 24	25 25 26	26 27 27	28 28 29	29 30 30	31 31 32	32
17 18 18	19 19 20	20 21 21	22 23 23	24 24 25	25 26 26	27 28 28	29 29 30	30 31 31	32 32 33	33
18 18 19	19 20 20	21 22 22	23 23 24	24 25 26	26 27 27	28 28 29	29 30 31	31 32 32	33 33 34	34
18 19 19	20 20 21	22 22 23	23 24 24	25 26 26	27 27 28	29 29 30	30 31 32	32 33 33	34 34 35	35
19 19 20	20 21 22	22 23 23	24 25 25	26 26 27	28 28 29	29 30 31	31 32 32	33 34 34	35 35 36	36
19 20 20	21 22 22	23 23 24	25 25 26	27 27 28	28 29 30	30 31 31	32 33 33	34 35 35	36 36 37	37
20 20 21	22 22 23	23 24 25	25 26 27	27 28 28	29 30 30	31 32 32	33 34 34	35 35 36	37 37 38	38
20 21 21	22 23 23	24 25 25	26 27 27	28 29 29	30 31 31	32 32 33	34 34 35	36 36 37	38 38 39	39
21 21 22	23 23 24	25 25 26	27 27 28	29 29 30	31 31 32	33 33 34	35 35 36	37 37 38	39 39 40	40
21 22 23	23 24 25	25 26 27	27 28 29	29 30 31	31 32 33	33 34 35	36 36 37	38 38 39	40 40 41	41
22 22 23	24 24 25	26 27 27	28 29 29	30 31 32	32 33 34	34 35 36	36 37 38	38 39 40	41 41 42	42
22 23 24	24 25 26	27 27 28	29 29 30	31 32 32	33 34 34	35 36 37	37 38 39	39 40 41	42 42 43	43
23 23 24	25 26 26	27 28 29	29 30 31	32 32 33	34 34 35	36 37 37	38 39 40	40 41 42	43 43 44	44
23 24 25	26 26 27	28 28 29	30 31 32	32 33 34	34 35 36	37 38 38	39 40 40	41 42 43	44 44 45	45
24 25 25	26 27 28	28 29 30	31 31 32	33 34 34	35 36 37	38 38 39	40 41 41	42 43 44	44 45 46	46
24 25 26	27 27 28	29 30 31	31 32 33	34 34 35	36 37 38	38 39 40	41 42 42	43 44 45	45 46 47	47
25 26 26	27 28 29	30 30 31	32 33 34	34 35 36	37 38 38	39 40 41	42 42 43	44 45 46	46 47 48	48
25 26 27	28 29 29	30 31 32	33 33 34	35 36 37	38 38 39	40 41 42	42 43 44	45 46 47	47 48 49	49
26 27 28	28 29 30	31 32 32	33 34 35	36 37 38	38 39 40	41 42 42	43 44 45	46 47 48	48 49 50	50
26 27 28	29 30 31	31 32 33	34 35 36	37 37 38	39 40 41	42 42 43	44 45 46	47 48 48	49 50 51	51
27 28 29	29 30 31	32 33 34	35 36 36	37 38 39	40 41 42	42 43 44	45 46 47	48 49 49	50 51 52	52
27 28 29	30 31 32	33 34 34	35 36 37	38 39 40	41 42 42	43 44 45	46 47 48	49 49 50	51 52 53	53
28 29 30	31 32 32	33 34 35	36 37 38	39 40 40	41 42 43	44 45 46	47 48 49	50 50 51	52 53 54	54
28 29 30	31 32 33	34 35 36	37 38 38	39 40 41	42 43 44	45 46 47	48 49 50	50 51 52	53 54 55	55
29 30 31	32 33 34	35 35 36	37 38 39	40 41 42	43 44 45	46 47 48	49 49 50	51 52 53	54 55 56	56
29 30 31	32 33 34	35 36 37	38 39 40	41 42 43	44 45 46	47 48 48	49 50 51	52 53 54	55 56 57	57
30 31 32	33 34 35	36 37 38	39 40 41	42 43 44	44 45 46	47 48 49	50 51 52	53 54 55	56 57 58	58
30 31 32	33 34 35	36 37 38	39 40 41	42 43 44	45 46 47	48 49 50	51 52 53	54 55 56	57 58 59	59

THE SUN SIGHT

Example 1: Falmouth Towards Bermuda 21 May 1991

Note we do not say 'to Bermuda' – that is regarded as tempting providence.

Log: Tuesday 21 May.
DR 49°23′N. 6°30′W.
Observed sextant altitude 44°03′ @ 15hr-23min-14sec.
Index error 2′ on the arc.
Height of eye 6ft (2m)

Working:	Time (GMT)			GHA	Declination
	hr	min	sec		
	14	- 00	- 00	30°52′.1	N.20°10′
Inc. for -	1	- 23	- 00	20°45′.0	
Inc. for -			14	3′.5	
	15	- 23	- 14	51°40′.6	
			minus W.long.	6°40′.6	
			LHA	45°	

Enter Tables with latitude, LHA and Dec.

	Hc	d	Z	
	43°57′ +	46	113°	Zn = 360 – 113 = 247°
d Corr.	08′			
	44°05′ Tabulated altitude			

Observed sextant altitude	44°03′
Index error 2′ on the arc	– 02′
Total Correction	+ 12′.7
True altitude	44°13′.7
Tabulated altitude	44°05′
Intercept	9′ towards (8′.7)

Plot: Chosen position 49°N. 6°40′.6W. Azimuth 247° Intercept 9′ towards.

That completes the observation, working and plotting. It only remains to draw the position line at right angles to the azimuth at the intercept point.

Just check the steps which we then need not follow so deeply in the second example.

Take the *Reed's Almanac* extract 3:37 (Fig 12) for Tuesday 21 May. The day starts at 0h, our midnight, when the Sun is opposite Greenwich so the GHA is nominally 180°. Actually, it is 180°52'.6 due to equation of time. The two-hour steps take us past noon to 14.00h where we extract the GHA of 30°52'.1 leaving 1h 23min 14s to account for. These inter-two-hour increments are given in *Reed's Almanac* 4:7 (Fig 13) which we now see. If you are into the second hour, take the third column which tells you what to add for hours and minutes – in our case 20°45' for 1h 23min. The first column deals with minutes or seconds, the second column is used for minutes and the fourth for seconds. In our case we take 3'.5 for 14s. So we have the total GHA for the time given to the second. Without offending the purists, *Reed's* is easier to use than the *Nautical Almanac* if you accept a slight dilution of accuracy as mentioned in the footnote to 4:7 (Fig 13). (About 400yd at occasional extreme times.)

When using *Reed's Almanac* 3:37 (Fig 12) for basic GHA it is convenient to extract declination given in the second column at the same time. Eyeball interpolation shows this to be N20°10' so we can exit the Almanac with GHA and declination as shown in Flowchart B (Fig 2).

Flowchart B shows that declination can go straight into the Tables but GHA must be converted to LHA to be digestible, and these are the rules of the game. We take our DR longitude and make the smallest change to it which will allow the LHA to be expressed in whole degrees and thus acceptable to the Tables, following the rule that west longitude is subtracted from the GHA and east longitude is added to it.

Take a simple case:

	GHA	36°40'	DR long. 13°20'W.
minus W. long.		13°40'	(Chosen long. 20' different)
LHA		23°00'	

Now try:

	GHA	36°10'	DR long. 45°50'W.
minus W. long.		46°10'	(Chosen long. 20' different
add 360° to GHA		396°10'	but we have changed the degrees.)
minus W. long.		46°10'	
LHA		350°00'	

Try an East long. Remember to *add* minutes to cancel out.

THE SUN SIGHT

	GHA	320°10′	DR long. 120°15′E.
plus E. long.		119°50′	(Chosen long. 25′ different.)
		440°00′	
minus		360°00′	
LHA		80°00′	

You cannot exceed 360° or go negative, so add or subtract 360 as required. The adjustment to DR long. need not exceed 30′ if you change the degree by one as shown. This is largely an artificial problem encountered in examinations, where DR longitude is **quoted** to a precision you never have in practice. On a yacht your knowledge of your DR is more vague, so you have more latitude with your longitude. (There must, I suppose, also be platitude and longitude!)

The Sight Reduction Tables
(Air Publication 3270)

From Flowchart B (Fig 2) you will see we enter these Tables with latitude, declination and LHA. With very little practice you will move swiftly through the selected page, and Table 5 (Fig 18) for declination adjustment. In fact, some navigators claim to beat calculators.

The Tables are supplied by HMSO and derive from joint work with the US Hydrographic Office. Volume 1 is devoted to stars and is a priceless masterpiece. Volume 2 covers Sun, Moon and planets for latitudes 0°–39°. Volume 3 covers the same bodies for latitudes 40°–89°.

The Tables are 'Promulgated for the information and guidance of all concerned', but respect the copyright rules. I have photocopied pages from my personal copies for certain limited trips where I carry my own navigational gear, and regard that as reasonable. There are about 1,000 certificated 'Ocean' Yachtmasters on the RYA Register and many yachts have these publications aboard.

We need to know how Volumes 2 and 3 are structured. Each whole degree of latitude throughout the range is covered, and in Volume 3 the declination is in two groups: from 0°–14° and from 15°–29°. Each group can be 'Same Name' as latitude (north or south) or 'Contrary Name'. In practice (say cruising off Brittany in summer) you will each day comfortably be on declination 15°–29° 'Same Name' as latitude. When you spread your wings and cruise oceans you will have to be careful, however, as some quite famous skippers have found.

For example, say you are just north of the equator in mid-March ('Contrary Name'), still north in late March ('Same Name' – declination now north), then you head south and cross the line ('Contrary Name').

Go back to Flowchart B (Fig 2) and the publication list on page 21, together with the worked Example 1. Refer to the extract from the Tables (Fig 16) and check that entering with the latitude 49° – LHA 45° – declination 20° we emerge with the Hc 43°57′, little *d* of + 46 and Z 113°. But the declination was 20°10′, not an even number of degrees like latitude and LHA. So we have to correct the tabulated altitude for these extra minutes, and this is achieved by the little *d* and Table 5 (Fig 18 – Tabulated Altitude Correction for Minutes of Declination). Simply run the *d* value of 46 at the head of Table 5 down to the 10′ for which we have to correct, and read 08′ which we add to Hc to get the tabulated altitude of 44°05′. After a few examples you will find you can do this in a few seconds.

The final trick is to check the azimuth, given as Z, which might or might not be the true azimuth, termed Zn. There are head and footnotes in the Tables which tell you how to deal with this. The head note says that in northern latitudes Z equals Zn if LHA exceeds 180°. But if less, you subtract Z from 360° to get Zn. You can do this entirely by rote, but think like this. In our case the azimuth could not be 113°. The Sun was in the south-west. By applying the rule we get 247°, which is logical. It is good practice to take the Sun's bearing at the time of sight as a deviation check: this and common sense will prevent confusion over the azimuth. The footnote dealing with south latitudes gives a different procedure.

There now follows a detailed explanation of the mysteries of Z and Zn. If you are happy to work by rote and drive straight down the flowchart, you can skip the following, but I know some readers will be curious and I don't recall it being covered elsewhere.

The Mysteries of Z and Zn

This complication arises because the Tables give azimuth as Z, but the true azimuth is Zn, explained as follows. The head and foot-notes in the Tables give four cases.

North latitude: LHA greater than 180° – Zn equals Z.
LHA less than 180° – Zn equals 360 minus Z.
South latitude: LHA greater than 180° – Zn equals 180 minus Z.
LHA less than 180° – Zn equals 180 plus Z.

THE SUN SIGHT

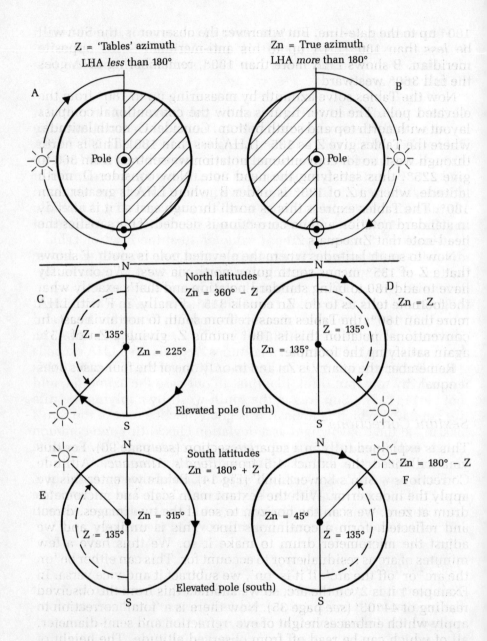

Fig 19   The mysteries of Z and Zn.

Fig 19 A and B show this 'less than/more than' 180° pictorially. In Fig 19 we are looking down on the pole, with the observer at the bottom. If the observer is at Greenwich, the Sun can be less than

180° up to the date-line. But wherever the observer is, the Sun will be *less* than 180° LHA up to his anti-meridian – his opposite meridian. B shows LHA more than 180°, remembering LHA goes the full 360° westward.

Now the Tables solve azimuth by measuring up to 180° from the elevated pole. The lower figures show the conventional compass layout with north top and south bottom. Consider C, north latitude, where the Tables give Z as 135° (LHA less than 180). This is north through west, so for conventional notation we subtract from 360 to give 225°, thus satisfying the head note. Now consider D, north latitude, where a Z of 135° is under B, where LHA is greater than 180°. The Tables express this as north through east so it is already in standard notation and no correction is needed. This satisfies the head-note that Zn equals Z.

Now to south latitudes where the elevated pole is south. E shows that a Z of 135° means south going north via west. We obviously have to add 180 to bring standard notation and that's exactly what the footnote tells us to do. Zn equals 315°. Finally, in F with LHA more than 180°, the Tables measure from south to north via east. In conventional notation this is 180° minus Z, giving a Zn of 45°, again satisfying the footnote.

Remember: the quarry is Zn and in only one of the four cases does it equal Z.

Sextant Corrections

This is explained fully in a separate section (*see* page 90). For this you will need the extract 4:5 from *Reed's Almanac*, 'Altitude Corrections – Sun's Lower Limb' (Fig 14). Before we enter this we apply the index error. With the sextant main scale and micrometer drum at zero, we scan the horizon to see if the two images, direct and reflected, form a continuous line. This is unlikely and we adjust the micrometer drum to make it so. We thus have a few minutes of arc as residual error to account for. This can either be 'on the arc' or 'off the arc'. If it is 'on', we subtract it and vice versa. In Example 1 it is 2′ on the arc, so we subtract this from the observed reading of 44°03′ (*see* page 35). Now there is a 'total' correction to apply which embraces height of eye, refraction and semi-diameter, all of which can be read off from observed altitude. The height of eye was 6′, so reading down from this to 44° gives 12′.7 to be added. The true altitude is therefore 44°13′.7 – call it 44°14′. We can now bring the two altitudes together (true and tabulated) as shown by the opposing arrows on Flowchart B (Fig 2) and derive 9′

as the intercept. True altitude was greater, so this is 'toward'.

Now we can complete the plot, using the intercept, the azimuth from the Tables, and the DR information lurking at the bottom of the flowchart. We plot the chosen position as 49°N. and 6°40′.6W. We choose this latitude because it is the nearest whole degree, and this longitude because it was DR longitude adjusted to give a whole degree of LHA. Now the azimuth is drawn through the chosen position at 247° and the intercept stepped off 9 miles on the latitude scale 'towards' the Sun. Then the position line is drawn at right angles to the azimuth at this point. (The flowchart shows an intercept of 5 miles 'away' but it is only pictorial.)

Example 2: South Coast Towards
L'Aberwrach 26 May 1991

Now take the second example in less detail. You use the same extracts as previously, but take page 63 of the Tables (Fig 17). This is a morning sight. You are on passage from the south coast of England to L'Aberwrach in May and get a morning shot. You will probably be operating in British Summer Time so the first thing to do is to knock off one hour to bring you to GMT. We all forget this at first.

Log: Sunday 26 May.
         DR 49°15′N.4°10′W.
         06h 45min 15s (GMT).
         Observed sextant altitude 20°27′.
         Height of eye 9ft (3m).
         Index error 3′ off.

	Time	GHA	Declination
Hours	06-00-00	270°46′.3	N21°03′
Minutes	45-00	11°15′.0	
Seconds	15	3′.8	
		282°05′.1	
minus West longitude		4°05′.1	
LHA		278°	

Hc	d	Z		Observed altitude	20°27′
20°50′	+ 43°	82°		Plus index error	03′
02′				Total correction	10′.5
20°52′	Intercept 11.5 away				20°40′.5

Plot: Chosen position 49°N. 4°05′W. Azimuth 82° Intercept 11.5. away.

So, in the case postulated we will have achieved a useful position line for our approach to L'Aberwrach, where we will dine well and relax for our trip down the Chenal du Four and South Brittany.

The Sextant

We now leave number crunching in order to deal with the prime tool of the astro-navigator's trade – the sextant (*see* Figs 20–8). I have firm views on the attitude to, and the use of, this instrument.

If you have read *Zen and the Art of Motor Cycle Maintenance* you will be ahead of me. You must be at peace with the sextant, even before you pick it up. Treat it as pianists are told to approach the Schumann A Minor Concerto – *allegro affettuoso*, or 'with affection'. This is not pure whimsy – it does make a difference.

The sextant is a well-developed optical instrument for measuring relative angles. In our context it measures the 'altitude' of a body. That is the angle of the body above the horizon, measured from the observer, using the horizon as horizontal reference. Any such tangent to the Earth's surface will do. A mountain lake with a horizon visible is O.K., and makes the point that height above sea level is unimportant in principle. For practice at home, you can use the reflected image of the body in a dish of water (artificial horizon). You halve the measured angle. Aircraft, at one time, used 'bubble sextants' but they do not work in yachts.

Let us remind ourselves of the objective. The 'altitude' is the first step toward the zenith distance, which we obtain by subtracting the sextant angle from 90°. This is the great circle distance from the geographical position (GP) of the body to the observer. This distance can be expressed in nautical miles or in degrees and minutes of arc. We use angular measure because the geometric figure to be solved is a spherical triangle whose three sides, as well as the 'included' angle, are expressed in arc.

There are many ways to describe the sextant; some are technically immaculate but somehow don't help. It is best to have an idea and then handle the sextant carefully. You will find a frame, with a swinging arm equipped with an integral mirror, which moves a pointer over an arc graduated in degrees. There is a coarse adjustment which 'de-clutches' the arc, and a fine micrometer adjuster which allows reading to part of a minute of arc.

You sight through a telescope or sighting tube and see a rectangular frame, half of which is clear glass through which you sight the horizon. The adjacent half is mirrored and allows you to

THE SUN SIGHT

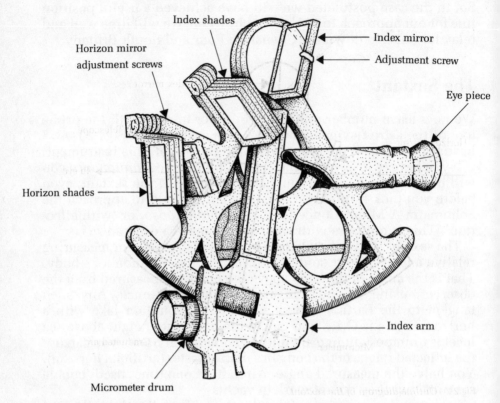

Index shades

Index mirror

Adjustment screw

Eye piece

Horizon mirror
adjustment screws

Horizon shades

Index arm

Micrometer drum

Fig 20   The sextant.

see the image reflected from the top mirror (the index mirror) and
bring it to the desired reference point directly seen through the
plain horizon glass. The sextant has been developed in detail but
not in principle – for instance, the two-part horizon glass can be
replaced by a single half-silvered mirror.

The brilliant optical concept of the basic sextant allows you to get
good altitude readings from a moving boat. It replaced previous
devices depending on hanging weights like astrolabes, improbable
devices like back staffs, and even coconut shells half-filled with
water and with sighting holes. I later show how a noon sight, with
the Sun at maximum altitude, can give a ship's latitude with a
simple calculation. For many years this *was* basic astro-navigation
– simply getting down, in most cases, to your desired latitude and
believing you knew enough to turn east or west, until you hit your
destination. This emphasizes the centuries of effort given to
measurement of altitude.

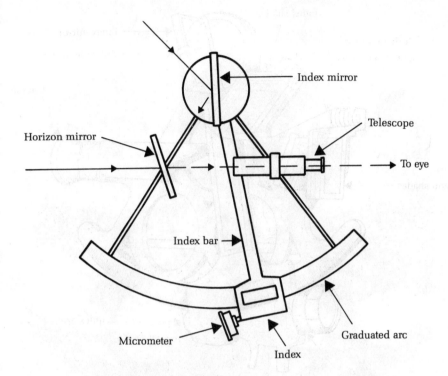

Fig 21   Outline diagram of the sextant.

How is It Set Up?

You will appreciate that the range will be roughly from 0°, with the body on the horizon, rising or setting, and up to 90° in the tropics with the Sun overhead. The optics decree that the angle between the first and last directions of the ray of light is double the angle between the mirrors (index and horizon). Although the sextant is so called because the arc is about one-sixth of a circle, it is calibrated to 120°. The mirrors are furnished with shades of various density to protect the eyes and enhance the sight, and also have various screw adjustments. When set up, the only error to affect us is the index error, because it cannot be entirely eliminated. (Attempts to do this are called 'tormenting' the sextant.)

Let us deal briefly with the others, realizing that each model can be different. Always consult the manufacturer's handbook. The index mirror has a simple check for perpendicularity to the frame.

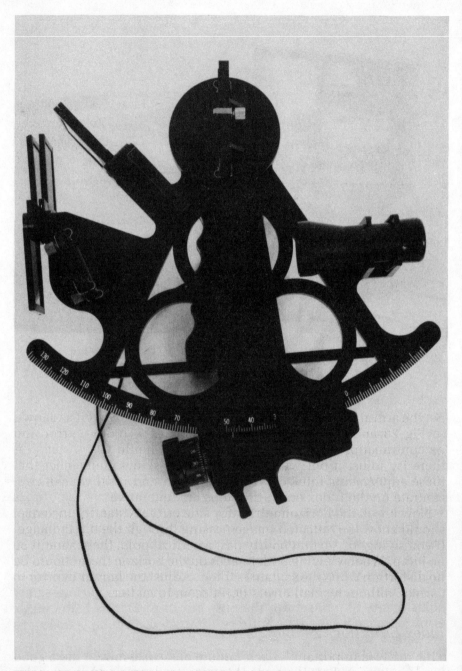

Fig 22 *The sextant has two index shades down, and one horizon shade. The reading is 47°27'. Use long line on micrometer drum.*

Fig 23 Perpendicularity of index mirror to frame. Ensure that reflected arc and actual arc are in line.

Set the arm at about 30° and remove the telescope. Hold it as shown in Fig 23 and view the arc as reflected in the index mirror and its continuation as viewed directly. There should be no step – if there is, adjust it out with the appropriate screw. Remember that these adjustments interact with each other, and until we can concentrate on the index error, the steps are reiterative.

Now check the horizon mirror for side error. A star, for instance, should show the reflected image passing through the direct image. If you swing the sextant bodily past a vertical pole, there should be no jump. When viewing both images on the horizon there should be no distortion when the sextant is tilted. Adjust the horizon mirror to correct, although small errors don't seem to matter.

Index Error (Figs 24 and 25)

This really is important – each minute of arc is a mile. Find a good hard horizon and set the sextant to zero on degree and micrometer scales. Look at the images. If there is no index error, the horizon

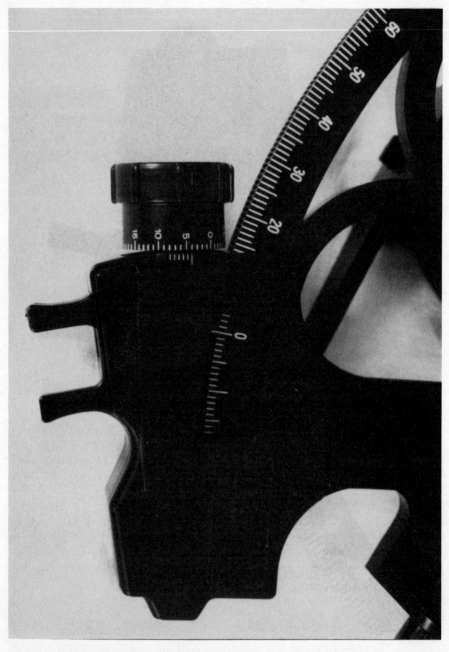

Fig 24   *Index error. This is 4' 'on' the arc. The micrometer drum has moved 4' on from zero with true and reflected images of horizon lined up. Subtract from sextant reading of Sun.*

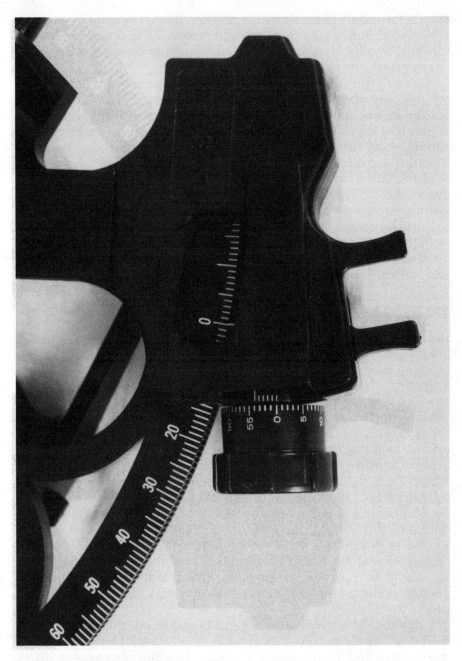

Fig 25   Index error. The reading is 54' which is 6' 'off' the arc. Micrometer
drum has been moved 6' back from zero to align horizons. Add this to Sun
reading.

should be a continuous line with no step. If not, bring them into line and read the micrometer to see the error. Get it down to about 3 minutes by adjusting the 'other' index mirror screw. Check if there is any effect on the perpendicularity setting.

Now you finish up with a small error which can be 'off' or 'on' the arc. Be clear about the distinction between 'error' and 'correction' – they are opposite! When you do the first sextant correction on the water, it is the index error. The others you have done and forgotten about. Make sure to check the index error *before every sight* and record it as, say, 3′ 'off' or 5′ 'on'. If 'off' you *add* to the observed reading, and if 'on' you *subtract*. People still get confused and I've been asked to include the kitchen scales example to illustrate the point (*see* Figs 26 and 27).

Whatever sight form you use it will say index error as the first sextant correction. Do not record it as plus or minus, as many forms do. That way leads to confusion. Simply say 'on the arc' or 'off the arc', or just 'on' or 'off'.

Taking the Sight

Here are some practical points. You will probably have an X3 telescope. If there is a swell or it is rough, remove it and use the sighting tube, or just the hole the scope would fit into. You will see a smaller, sharper Sun and avoid the queasiness that often accompanies using magnifying devices like binoculars on a rolling yacht.

More important, don't operate the sextant in the classical way unless you have to snatch a sight in passing cloud. The standard drill is to bring the Sun's lower limb to rest momentarily on the horizon whilst 'rocking' the sextant to make sure it is upright, in effect. Then check the time to a few seconds. The rocking is open to misinterpretation. You rotate and oscillate the sextant about its vertical centre. You can imagine that if it were not vertical the Sun would be further from the horizon, and setting it down would give a false high reading. It is very difficult to 'rock' and adjust the micrometer at the same time, and I find this hopeless and unnecessary in practice. It leads to taking numerous sights, and averaging them simply because you have no confidence in any of them.

You should know whether a sight is good, and this is how to do it. If it is morning, before local noon, the Sun will be rising. Get a rough idea and then plunge the Sun with the micrometer drum about its diameter below the horizon. Now you can 'rock' to your heart's content; just watch the Sun rising – it won't take long – and

Fig 26   Index error. Scales read 50g, which is 'off the arc'.

Fig 27   Index error. 1kg of sugar weighs 50g low. Add the index error to correct.

THE SUN SIGHT

Fig 28 Handling the sextant – one index shade down, no horizon shade. Try keeping both eyes open.

when the lower limb kisses the horizon, take the time. When you plunge the Sun down, you usually have time to set to a convenient reading, like a precise minute setting. Some people try to set to a value which makes a precise number, absorbing the index error, but I don't favour that.

Now take an afternoon sight, when the Sun is falling. This time you flick the adjustment up to get the Sun a reasonable height *above* the horizon. Then wait for the lower limb to descend and kiss the horizon, whilst performing the 'rocking' act. This way you are doing one controllable thing at a time and are likely to get sights you could bet your boots on. When taking the time, unless single-handed, the classic thing is to shout 'Now!', hoping your crew will produce an immaculate timing. What usually happens is that the response is 'What?', leading to some strained discussions, or you get a totally implausible number. It is best to do it yourself. You can wear your watch on the inside of your wrist for easy reading, or follow my practice which is heretical but works. I simply allow three seconds for carefully lowering the sextant and reading my watch. It seems consistent. A friend of mine has a stopwatch fitted to his sextant and, of course, if you zero it at midnight, you have got it made.

When you take your data to the chart table you will also need height of eye. This figures in the calculations. You will have decided where to take your sights from. Make yourself firm from the waist down and flexible in the arms and shoulders. You need to be high enough to get the horizon above the swell, but not so you compromise stability and safety. Height of eye is usually about 6ft (2m) above the water. Some masters of detail record the height of eye for various positions in the boat and select the best for prevailing conditions. Never take sights if the horizon is not sharp. It is a temptation – a gross error shows up, but what confidence can you have in the observation anyway?

So when you eventually take your gear and records down to the chart table you will have: the precious sextant with the lanyard round your neck; your Sight Book or Deck Book with the observed reading; index error; height of eye; GMT time; and a hand bearing-compass reading of the body at time of sight. This is one observation which you can farm out. You now need further corrections from *Reed's Almanac* to get true sextant altitude and reach the nodal point on flowchart B (Fig 2) where you compare this with tabulated altitude to get intercept.

Now, please consult *Reed's Almanac*, page 91, 4:5 (Fig 14). Before entering this Table, you will have corrected the sextant altitude for index error, thus arriving at observed altitude. It is very simple. You enter with height of eye and observed altitude, emerging with the correction in minutes, which you always add. Note the monthly correction at the bottom of the page. If submitting work to the RYA or any other examining body, do not omit mention of this, even if it is zero, as they need to know that you know about it. It corrects for changing semi-diameter of the Sun, and is regarded in some quarters as negligible. Now, we brought the lower limb of the Sun down to the horizon but the mathematics require the centre of the Sun, which is difficult to find. So we take the lower limb, which is easier, and correct it. The correction is obviously positive and would amount to about 15′ (the same as the Moon, actually), but other corrections are negative, so we finish up with about plus 12′. In fact, *in extremis*, you could use 12′, as some trawler skippers did years ago.

THE SUN SIGHT

So what are the other corrections? Height of eye causes the horizon to dip away and is called 'dip'. Dip increases the measured angle, so the correction is negative. The general result of the observed altitude correction is negative also and accounts for refraction of the atmosphere. This is negligible with the Sun overhead, but increases as it drops to the horizon because there is more atmosphere through which to look.

Example: A Sun Sight in the Ionian Sea

As a 'live' example of an actual sight, take the sight shown in Fig 29. This was a passage from St Cyprien to Bodrum – about 1,400 miles accomplished in 11 days. Now, some people are slightly condescending about trips in the Mediterranean, but we had minimal navigation gear and depended on astro-navigation. The depth sounder is limited as the chart shows depths of something like

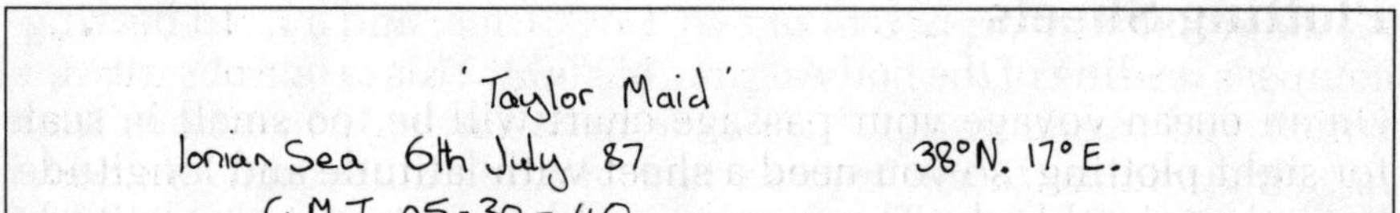

'Taylor Maid'

Ionian Sea 6th July 87   38°N. 17°E.

GMT 05-30-40

Time	GHA	Sext 19°–39'
04-00	238° 51'	+ Ind.Error –02'
1·30	22° 30'	+ Tot. Corr –11'
40 secs	10'	True Alt 19°– 52'
	261° 31'	
+E Long	16° 29'	
LHA	278° – 00'	Dec N.22° 45'

Hc   d   Z
19°– 25'   +33   77°
        25'   Plot
Tab. Alt. 19°–50'   38°N. 16°– 29'E.
True Alt. 19 – 52'   AZ 077° Intercept ·02' Towards

Fig 29 Log entry for Taylor Maid.

4,000m in places. RDF bearings are unreliable. I know the tides are negligible, but on legs of 300–400 miles the current is not. The tidal atlas is hard to analyse and a cross-current of a fraction of a knot can be significant on such legs. Hazy horizons were sometimes a problem, but the crew alerted me when they cleared. The nights were marvellous and navigation was a pure joy.

All the procedures discussed so far are embraced in this simple working (Fig 29). I used extracts from A.P. 3270, Volume 2, as Volume 3 stops at latitude 40°. The splendid Tables in *Reed's Almanac* make short work of the GHA and sextant corrections.

Note that east longitude is added to GHA to get LHA. Because the LHA exceeds 180°, Zn equals Z, so the 77° from the Tables gives Zn directly.

I did not use a formatted sight form because simple Sun shots are treated in the three obvious 'blocks' and it becomes second nature. I am not against sight forms in general, but only those which cater for so many possibilities that they create an elaborate puzzle when a simple task and layout is quite obvious.

Plotting Sheets

On an ocean voyage your passage chart will be too small in scale for sight plotting, so you need a sheet with latitude and longitude, but otherwise blank. The simple problem is to get the latitude/longitude scales right, their proportion being different for different latitudes. Chart agents will provide plotting sheets with a range of scales, and you have to delete those not required. They are a bit large for yachts and are likely to be phased out eventually.

When you are cruising the usual European waters, and trying out some Sun sights, you might well have some charts aboard you can use for practice. Apart from Admiralty charts which may be suitable (that is, having a convenient parallel of latitude) you might have Imray or Stanford charts which satisfy the purpose. The British Hydrographic Department has announced its intention to increase the numbers of chart co-ordinates so that the latitude/longitude lines will close up. This will be a help.

It is comparatively easy to generate plotting sheets on A4 paper. Some people make heavy weather of it but it is basically simple. You will be aware that except at the equator the longitude scale is smaller than the latitude scale. In fact, the longitude is the cosine of the latitude, and you can derive the scale difference by punching the cosine button on your calculator for the required latitude. In

LHA	15° Hc d Z	16° Hc d Z	17° Hc d Z	18° Hc d Z	19° Hc d Z	20° Hc d Z	21° Hc d Z
70	24 49 +34 90	25 23 +35 89	25 58 +33 88	26 31 +34 87	27 05 +33 86	27 38 +33 85	28 11 +32 84
71	24 02 34 89	24 36 34 89	25 10 34 88	25 44 34 87	26 18 33 86	26 51 33 85	27 24 32 84
72	23 14 35 89	23 49 34 88	24 23 34 87	24 57 34 86	25 31 33 85	26 04 33 84	26 37 32 83
73	22 27 35 88	23 02 34 87	23 36 35 86	24 10 34 86	24 44 33 85	25 17 33 84	25 50 33 83
74	21 40 34 88	22 14 35 87	22 49 34 86	23 23 34 85	23 57 33 84	24 30 33 83	25 03 33 82
75	20 53 +34 87	21 27 +35 86	22 02 +34 85	22 36 +34 84	23 10 +33 83	23 43 +33 83	24 16 +33 82
76	20 05 35 86	20 40 35 86	21 15 34 85	21 49 34 84	22 23 33 83	22 56 34 82	23 30 32 81
77	19 18 35 86	19 53 35 85	20 28 34 84	21 02 34 83	21 36 33 82	22 09 34 82	22 43 33 80
78	18 31 35 85	19 06 35 84	19 41 34 83	20 15 34 83	20 49 34 82	21 23 33 81	21 56 34 80
79	17 44 35 85	18 19 35 84	18 54 34 83	19 28 34 82	20 02 34 81	20 36 34 80	21 10 33 79
80	16 57 +35 84	17 32 +35 83	18 07 +34 82	18 41 +35 81	19 16 34 81	19 50 +33 80	20 23 +34 79
81	16 10 35 83	16 45 35 83	17 20 35 82	17 55 34 81	18 29 34 80	19 03 34 79	19 37 34 78
82	15 23 35 83	15 58 35 82	16 33 35 81	17 08 34 80	17 42 35 79	18 17 34 79	18 51 34 78
83	14 36 35 82	15 11 35 81	15 46 35 81	16 21 35 80	16 56 34 79	17 30 35 78	18 05 34 77
84	13 49 36 82	14 25 35 81	15 00 35 80	15 35 35 79	16 10 34 78	16 44 35 77	17 19 34 77
85	13 03 +35 81	13 38 +35 80	14 13 +35 79	14 48 +35 79	15 23 +35 78	15 58 +35 77	16 33 +34 76
86	12 16 36 80	12 52 35 79	13 27 35 79	14 02 35 78	14 37 35 77	15 12 35 76	15 47 34 75
87	11 29 36 80	12 05 36 79	12 41 35 78	13 16 35 77	13 51 35 77	14 26 35 76	15 01 35 75
88	10 43 36 79	11 19 35 78	11 54 36 78	12 30 35 77	13 05 36 76	13 41 35 75	14 16 34 74
89	09 56 36 79	10 32 36 78	11 08 36 77	11 44 36 76	12 20 35 75	12 55 35 75	13 30 35 74
90	09 10 +36 78	09 46 +36 77	10 22 +36 77	10 58 +36 76	11 34 +35 75	12 09 +36 74	12 45 +35 73
91	08 24 36 78	09 00 36 77	09 36 36 76	10 12 36 75	10 48 36 74	11 24 36 73	12 00 35 73
92	07 38 36 77	08 14 37 76	08 51 36 75	09 27 36 75	10 03 36 74	10 39 36 73	11 15 35 72
93	06 52 36 76	07 28 37 76	08 05 36 75	08 41 36 74	09 17 37 73	09 54 36 72	10 30 36 72
94	06 06 37 76	06 43 36 75	07 19 37 74	07 56 36 73	08 32 37 73	09 09 36 72	09 45 36 71
95	05 20 +37 75	05 57 +37 74	06 34 +37 74	07 11 +36 73	07 47 +37 72	08 24 +36 71	09 00 +37 70
96	04 35 37 75	05 12 37 74	05 49 37 73	06 26 36 72	07 02 37 71	07 39 37 71	08 16 36 70
97	03 49 37 74	04 26 38 73	05 04 37 72	05 41 37 72	06 18 37 71	06 55 37 70	07 32 36 69
98	03 04 37 73	03 41 38 73	04 19 37 72	04 56 37 71	05 33 37 70	06 10 38 69	06 48 37 69
99	02 18 38 73	02 56 38 72	03 34 37 71	04 11 38 70	04 49 37 69	05 26 38 69	06 04 37 68
100	01 33 +38 72	02 11 +38 71	02 49 +38 71	03 27 +37 70	04 04 +38 69	04 42 +38 68	05 20 +37 67
101	00 49 38 71	01 27 38 71	02 05 37 70	02 42 38 69	03 20 38 68	03 58 38 68	04 36 38 67
102	00 04 38 71	00 42 38 70	01 20 38 69	01 58 39 69	02 37 38 68	03 15 38 67	03 53 38 66
103	−0 41 39 70	−0 02 38 69	00 36 38 69	01 14 39 68	01 53 39 67	02 31 39 66	03 10 38 66
104	−1 25 38 70	−0 47 39 69	−0 08 39 68	00 31 38 67	01 09 39 67	01 48 39 66	02 27 38 65
105	−2 09 +38 69	−1 31 +39 68	−0 52 +39 67	−0 13 +39 67	00 26 +39 66	01 05 +39 65	01 44 +39 64
106	−2 54 40 69	−2 14 39 68	−1 35 39 67	−0 56 39 66	−0 17 39 66	00 22 39 65	01 01 40 64
107	−3 37 39 68	−2 58 39 67	−2 19 40 66	−1 39 39 65	−1 00 40 65	−0 20 39 64	00 19 39 63
108	−4 21 40 67	−3 41 39 66	−3 02 40 66	−2 22 40 65	−1 42 39 64	−1 03 40 63	−0 23 40 63
109	−5 05 40 66	−4 25 40 66	−3 45 40 65	−3 05 40 64	−2 25 40 64	−1 45 40 63	−1 05 40 62
110	−5 48 +40 66	−5 08 +40 65	−4 28 +41 64	−3 47 +40 64	−3 07 +40 63	−2 27 +40 62	−1 47 +41 61
111		−5 50 40 64					−2 28 41 61
112			−5 52 40 63				−3 09 41 60
113				−5 53 41 62			−3 50 41 59
114					−5 53 41 60		−4 30 41 59
115						−5 53 +42 59	−5 11 +42 58
116							−5 51 42 58
117							

LHA	15°	16°	17°	18°	19°	20°	21°
86	−6 06 37 104 274						
85	−5 20 −37 105	−5 57 +37 106 275					
84	−4 35 37 105	−5 12 37 106	−5 49 37 107	−6 26 36 108 276			
83	−3 49 37 106	−4 26 38 107	−5 04 37 108	−5 41 37 108	−6 18 37 109 277		
82	−3 04 37 107	−3 41 38 107	−4 19 37 108	−4 56 37 109	−5 33 37 110	−6 10 38 111 278	
81	−2 18 38 107	−2 56 38 108	−3 34 37 109	−4 11 38 110	−4 49 37 110	−5 26 38 111	−6 04 37 112
80	−1 33 −38 108	−2 11 −38 109	−2 49 −38 109	−3 27 −37 110	−4 04 −38 111	−4 42 −38 112	−5 20 −37 113
79	−0 49 38 109	−1 27 38 109	−2 05 37 110	−2 42 38 111	−3 20 38 112	−3 58 38 112	−4 36 38 113
78	−0 04 38 109	−0 42 38 110	−1 20 38 111	−1 58 38 111	−2 37 38 112	−3 15 38 113	−3 53 38 114
77	00 41 39 110	00 02 38 111	−0 36 38 111	−1 14 39 112	−1 53 38 113	−2 31 39 114	−3 10 38 114
76	01 25 38 110	00 47 38 111	00 08 39 112	−0 31 38 113	−1 09 39 113	−1 48 39 114	−2 27 38 115
75	02 09 −38 111	01 31 −39 112	00 52 −39 113	00 13 −39 113	−0 26 −39 114	−1 05 −39 115	−1 44 −39 116
74	02 54 40 112	02 14 39 112	01 35 39 113	00 56 39 114	00 17 39 115	−0 22 39 115	−1 01 40 116
73	03 37 39 112	02 58 39 113	02 19 40 114	01 39 39 115	01 00 40 115	00 20 39 116	−0 19 39 117
72	04 21 40 113	03 41 39 114	03 02 40 114	02 22 40 115	01 42 39 116	01 03 40 117	00 23 40 117
71	05 05 40 114	04 25 40 114	03 45 40 115	03 05 40 116	02 25 40 117	01 45 40 117	01 05 40 118
70	05 48 −40 114	05 08 −40 115	04 28 −41 116	03 47 −40 116	03 07 −40 117	02 27 −40 118	01 47 −41 119

Fig 30   Declination (15°–29°) Same Name as Latitude.

LAT 38°

Each cell: Hc d Z

22°	23°	24°	25°	26°	27°	28°	29°	LHA
28 43 +32 84	29 15 +32 83	29 47 +31 82	30 18 +30 81	30 48 +31 80	31 19 +29 79	31 48 +29 78	32 17 +29 77	290
27 56 32 83	28 28 32 82	29 00 31 81	29 31 31 80	30 02 30 79	30 32 30 78	31 02 30 77	31 32 28 76	289
27 09 33 82	27 42 31 81	28 13 32 80	28 45 31 79	29 16 30 79	29 46 30 78	30 16 30 77	30 46 29 76	288
26 23 32 82	26 55 32 81	27 27 31 80	27 58 31 79	28 29 31 78	29 00 30 77	29 30 30 76	30 00 29 75	287
25 36 32 81	26 08 32 80	26 40 32 79	27 12 31 78	27 43 31 77	28 14 30 76	28 44 30 76	29 14 30 75	286
24 49 +33 81	25 22 +32 80	25 54 +32 79	26 26 +31 78	26 57 +31 77	27 28 +31 76	27 59 +30 75	28 29 +30 74	285
24 02 33 80	24 35 32 79	25 07 32 78	25 39 32 77	26 11 31 76	26 42 31 75	27 13 30 74	27 43 31 74	284
23 16 33 80	23 49 32 79	24 21 32 78	24 53 32 77	25 25 32 76	25 57 31 75	26 28 30 74	26 58 30 73	283
22 30 32 79	23 02 33 78	23 35 32 77	24 07 32 76	24 39 32 75	25 11 31 74	25 42 31 73	26 13 31 73	282
21 43 33 78	22 16 33 78	22 49 32 77	23 21 33 76	23 54 31 75	24 25 32 74	24 57 31 73	25 28 31 72	281
20 57 +33 78	21 30 +33 77	22 03 +33 76	22 36 +32 75	23 08 +32 74	23 40 +32 73	24 12 +31 72	24 43 +31 72	280
20 11 33 77	20 44 33 76	21 17 33 76	21 50 33 75	22 23 32 74	22 55 32 73	23 27 31 72	23 58 32 71	279
19 25 33 77	19 58 33 76	20 31 34 75	21 05 32 74	21 37 33 73	22 10 32 72	22 42 32 71	23 14 31 71	278
18 39 33 76	19 12 34 75	19 46 33 75	20 19 33 74	20 52 33 73	21 25 32 72	21 57 32 71	22 29 32 70	277
17 53 34 76	18 27 33 75	19 00 34 74	19 34 33 73	20 07 33 72	20 40 33 71	21 13 32 70	21 45 32 70	276
17 07 +34 75	17 41 +34 74	18 15 +34 73	18 49 +33 73	19 22 +33 72	19 55 +33 71	20 28 +34 70	21 01 +32 69	275
16 21 35 75	16 56 34 73	17 30 34 73	18 04 33 72	18 37 34 71	19 11 33 70	19 44 33 69	20 17 32 69	274
15 36 34 74	16 10 35 73	16 45 34 72	17 19 34 71	17 53 33 71	18 26 34 70	19 00 33 69	19 33 33 68	273
14 50 35 73	15 25 35 73	16 00 34 72	16 34 34 71	17 08 34 70	17 42 34 69	18 16 33 69	18 49 33 67	272
14 05 35 73	14 40 35 72	15 15 34 71	15 49 35 70	16 24 34 70	16 58 34 69	17 32 33 68	18 05 34 67	271
13 20 +35 72	13 55 +35 72	14 30 +35 71	15 05 +35 70	15 40 +34 69	16 14 +34 68	16 48 +34 67	17 22 +34 66	270
12 35 35 72	13 10 36 71	13 46 35 70	14 21 34 69	14 55 35 68	15 30 35 68	16 05 34 67	16 39 34 66	269
11 50 36 71	12 26 35 70	13 01 35 70	13 36 36 69	14 12 34 68	14 46 35 67	15 21 35 66	15 56 34 65	268
11 06 35 71	11 41 36 70	12 17 36 69	12 53 35 68	13 28 35 67	14 03 35 67	14 38 35 66	15 13 34 65	267
10 21 36 70	10 57 36 69	11 33 36 69	12 09 35 68	12 44 36 67	13 20 35 66	13 55 35 65	14 30 35 64	266
09 37 +36 70	10 13 +36 69	10 49 +36 68	11 25 +36 67	12 01 +36 66	12 37 +35 65	13 12 +36 65	13 48 +35 64	265
08 52 37 69	09 29 36 68	10 05 37 67	10 42 36 67	11 18 36 66	11 54 36 65	12 30 35 64	13 05 36 63	264
08 08 37 68	08 45 37 68	09 22 36 67	09 58 37 66	10 35 36 65	11 11 36 64	11 47 36 64	12 23 36 63	263
07 25 37 68	08 02 36 67	08 38 37 66	09 15 37 65	09 52 36 65	10 28 37 64	11 05 36 63	11 41 36 62	262
06 41 37 67	07 18 37 67	07 55 37 66	08 32 37 65	09 09 37 64	09 46 37 63	10 23 37 62	11 00 36 61	261
05 57 +38 67	06 35 +37 66	07 12 +38 65	07 50 +37 64	08 27 +37 64	09 04 +37 63	09 41 +37 62	10 18 +37 61	260
05 14 38 66	05 52 38 65	06 30 37 65	07 07 38 64	07 45 37 63	08 22 37 62	08 59 38 61	09 37 37 61	259
04 31 38 65	05 09 38 65	05 47 38 64	06 25 38 63	07 03 37 63	07 40 38 62	08 18 38 61	08 56 37 60	258
03 48 38 65	04 26 39 64	05 05 38 63	05 43 38 63	06 21 38 62	06 59 38 61	07 37 38 60	08 15 38 59	257
03 05 39 64	03 44 38 64	04 22 39 63	05 01 38 62	05 39 38 61	06 18 38 60	06 56 38 60	07 34 38 59	256
02 23 +39 64	03 02 +39 63	03 40 +39 62	04 19 +39 61	04 58 +39 61	05 37 +38 60	06 15 +39 59	06 54 +38 58	255
01 41 39 63	02 20 39 62	02 59 39 62	03 38 39 61	04 17 39 60	04 56 39 59	05 35 39 59	06 14 39 58	254
00 58 40 62	01 38 39 62	02 17 40 61	02 57 39 61	03 36 39 60	04 15 40 59	04 55 39 58	05 34 39 57	253
00 17 39 62	00 56 40 61	01 36 40 60	02 16 39 60	02 55 40 59	03 35 40 58	04 15 39 57	04 54 40 57	252
-0 25 40 61	00 15 40 61	00 55 40 60	01 35 40 59	02 15 40 58	02 55 40 57	03 35 40 57	04 15 40 56	251
-1 06 +40 61	-0 26 +41 60	00 14 +41 59	00 55 +40 58	01 35 +40 57	02 15 +41 57	02 56 +40 56	03 36 +40 55	250
-1 47 40 60	-1 07 41 59	-0 26 41 59	00 15 40 58	00 55 41 57	01 36 40 56	02 16 41 56	02 57 41 55	249
-2 28 41 59	-1 47 41 59	-1 06 41 58	-0 25 41 57	00 16 41 56	00 57 41 55	01 38 41 55	02 19 41 54	248
-3 09 42 59	-2 27 41 58	-1 46 41 57	-1 05 41 57	-0 24 42 56	00 15 41 54	00 59 41 54	01 40 42 54	247
-3 49 42 58	-3 07 41 57	-2 26 42 57	-1 44 41 56	-1 03 42 55	-0 21 42 54	00 21 41 54	01 02 42 53	246
-4 29 +42 57	-3 47 +42 57	-3 05 +42 56	-2 23 +42 55	-1 41 +42 55	-0 59 +42 54	-0 17 +42 53	00 25 +42 52	245
-5 09 43 57	-4 28 42 56	-3 44 42 55	-3 02 42 55	-2 20 43 54	-1 37 42 53	-0 55 42 53	-0 13 43 52	244
-5 48 42 56	-5 06 43 55	-4 23 43 55	-3 40 42 54	-2 58 43 53	-2 15 43 53	-1 32 43 52	-0 49 42 51	243
118	-5 44 43 55	-5 01 43 54	-4 18 43 53	-3 35 43 53	-2 52 43 52	-2 09 43 51	-1 26 43 51	242
	119	-5 40 44 53	-4 56 43 53	-4 13 44 52	-3 29 43 51	-2 46 43 51	-2 03 44 50	241
		120	-5 34 +44 52	-4 50 +44 51	-4 06 +44 51	-3 22 +43 50	-2 39 +44 49	240
		121	-6 11 44 51	-5 27 44 51	-4 43 45 50	-3 58 44 49	-3 14 44 49	239
			122	-6 03 44 50	-5 19 45 49	-4 34 44 49	-3 50 45 48	238
				123	-5 54 45 49	-5 10 45 48	-4 25 45 47	237
					124	-5 45 46 47	-4 59 45 47	236
						125	-5 33 +45 46	235
						126	-6 07 46 45	234

279

22°	23°	24°	25°	26°	27°	28°	29°	LHA
-5 57 -38 113								280
-5 14 38 114	-5 52 38 115							281
-4 31 38 115	-5 09 38 115	-5 47 38 116						282
-3 48 38 115	-4 26 39 116	-5 05 38 117	-5 43 38 117	-6 21 38 118				283
-3 05 39 116	-3 44 38 116	-4 22 39 117	-5 01 38 118	-5 39 39 119	-6 18 38 120			284
-2 23 -39 116	-3 02 -38 117	-3 40 -39 118	-4 19 -39 119	-4 58 -39 119	-5 37 -38 120	-6 15 -39 121		285
-1 41 39 117	-2 20 39 118	-2 59 39 118	-3 38 39 119	-4 17 39 120	-4 56 39 121	-5 35 39 121	-6 14 39 122	286
-0 58 39 118	-1 38 39 118	-2 17 40 119	-2 57 39 120	-3 36 39 121	-4 15 40 121	-4 55 39 122	-5 34 39 123	287
-0 17 39 118	-0 56 39 119	-1 36 40 119	-2 15 40 120	-2 55 40 121	-3 35 40 122	-4 15 39 123	-4 54 40 123	288
00 25 40 119	-0 15 40 119	-0 55 40 120	-1 35 40 121	-2 15 40 122	-2 55 40 122	-3 35 40 123	-4 15 40 124	289
01 06 -40 119	00 26 -40 120	-0 14 -41 121	-0 55 -40 122	-1 35 -40 122	-2 15 -41 123	-2 56 -40 124	-3 36 -40 125	290

| 22° | 23° | 24° | 25° | 26° | 27° | 28° | 29° |

CONTRARY NAME TO LATITUDE

THE SUN SIGHT

SIGHT FORM

IONIAN SEA

Vessel TAYLOR MAID   **Date** 6-7-87   **DR Lat** 38°N.   **Long** 17°E.

(GMT) Time 05-30-40   **Compass Bearing** —   **(Body)** Sun

(GMT) TIME		GHA	Dec.		Sextant	
Hours	04-00	238°-51′	N.22°-45′	**Obs.**	19°-39′	✓
Hr/Min	1-30	22°-30′		**Index**	-02′	**(Off/On)**
Secs	40	-10′		**Corr.**	-11′	**+ −**
Total	05-30-40	261°-31′		**True Alt.**	19°-52′	
Assumed Long.		16°-29′		**Tab. Alt.**	19°-50′	
(Minus W. plus E.)				**Intercept**	-02′	**(To/away)**
LHA		278°-00′				

TABLES	Chosen Lat	38°			PLOT	
Hc	**d**	**Z**	**Azimuth**	**Chosen Position**		38°N.16°-29′E.
19°-25	+ 33	77°	77°	**Azimuth**		077°
-25	(*d* corr.)			**Intercept**		-02 TOWARDS
Tab. Alt.	19°-50′			**Position Line**		✓

Fig 31   Sight form.

latitude 45° this is 0.7, so if it suits you to give the latitude scale 1in for 10 minutes, then your longitude scale is $^7/_{10}$ in for 10 minutes. You can, of course, pinch the scales from any large-scale chart covering the latitude required.

By far the simplest solution involves two lines on a sheet of graph paper. Just draw a horizontal line about midway up the sheet and mark it as the required latitude. From one end, draw a diagonal line at the latitude angle. This is your latitude and distance scale. Using this system, the longitude scale is arbitrary and you can mark, say, 10 minutes of longitude to fit the heavy vertical lines on the graph. In west longitude draw the diagonal from the right end of the horizontal line, because the numbers increase to the left (Fig 32). In east longitude, draw from the left end as numbers increase to the right (Fig 33).

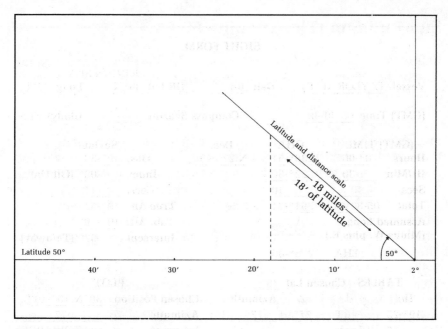

Fig 32 Plotting sheet – west long.

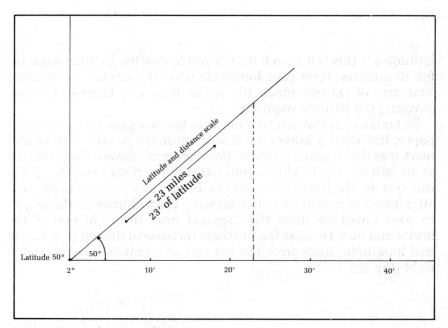

Fig 33 Plotting sheet – east long.

THE SUN SIGHT

Sun-Run-Sun (The Running Fix)

Before I conclude Part One with a review of the Sun sight steps, the reader should be clear as to the use of the position line obtained. It is not a fix in itself, just a line the yacht was on at the time of sight, like any other single position line.

It is too advanced at this stage to consider multiple sights where Sun, Moon, planets or stars offer a selection of sights from which three or four taken almost simultaneously can give a fix. So we find two broad paths to follow. We can cross the Sun's position line with a line or bearing from another source, such as an RDF bearing. This can be useful when practising sights in your usual cruising area, where the opportunities exist. The other path is the running fix which caters for sights taken at different times, from the same or a different source.

The Sun-Run-Sun concept is a running fix. You take a sight; then from the position line obtained you run the course and distance to the next sight and derive its position line. Now, move the first position line bodily (that is parallel) forward to run through your DR position at the second fix. The two position lines will cross and that is your fix.

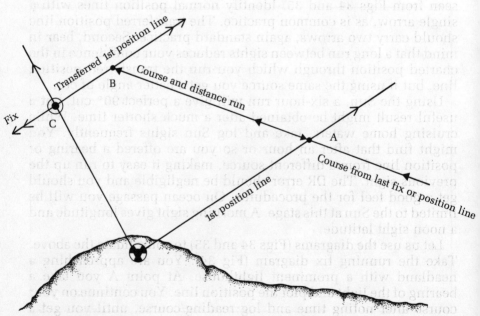

Fig 34   *The running fix.*

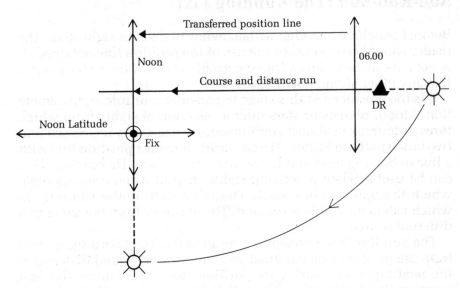

Fig 35   Sun-Run-Sun.

There are just a few points to make on this, and these are better seen from Figs 34 and 35. Identify normal position lines with a single arrow, as is common practice. The transferred position line should carry two arrows, again standard practice. Second, bear in mind that a long run between sights reduces your confidence in the charted position through which you run the transferred position line, but if using the same source you get a better angle of cut.

Using the Sun, a six-hour run will give a perfect 90° cut, but a useful result might be obtained after a much shorter time. While cruising home waters, take and log Sun sights frequently. You might find that after an hour or so you are offered a bearing or position line from a different source, making it easy to run up the previous sight. The DR error should be negligible and you should get a good feel for the procedures. On ocean passage you will be limited to the Sun at this stage. A morning sight gives longitude and a noon sight latitude.

Let us use the diagrams (Figs 34 and 35) to consolidate the above. Take the running fix diagram (Fig 34). You are approaching a headland with a prominent lighthouse. At point A you take a bearing of the light and plot the position line. You continue on your course after noting time and log reading/course, until you get a good angle of cut. Then take a second bearing, again with time and log reading. From any sensible point at A, run up course and distance and mark its termination at B. Now transfer the first position line to run through B, and where it cuts the second position line is your fix. If you had selected A nearer the light so that B met at C, the figure would have been true!

Now take the Sun-Run-Sun diagram (Fig 35). You are in mid-Atlantic heading west. It is early morning, the Sun is in the east and you get a sight. The azimuth will be 090° so the position line, being at right angles, will be north–south, giving a useful line of longitude. Your DR is shown by the yacht, but you now know you are ahead of that so move it up to the position line, again your Most Probable Position. Carry on your declared course until noon when you take another sight. The Sun will now be south and the position line east–west, giving a latitude. This shows you are south of your DR course. Now transfer the morning position line forward by the course and distance run, marking it with double arrows to avoid confusion. Where this intersects your noon latitude is your noon position.

It is traditional to establish your daily position at noon. This is local noon when the Sun is due south. You can take a later sight, giving you another longitude, and run this back to noon as a cross-check. The noon sight has special significance as it can give a latitude very simply, in theory. This is discussed later. If you are in fair weather and have the option, you can arrange sights to suit your course – a beam position line will give you distance and dead ahead will give you course.

The Noon Sight for Latitude

Fig 6 (page 17) shows the navigational triangle PZX which we analyse later, as it is not 'need to know' for Part One. However, at local noon the Sun is due south, and the yacht and the geographical position (GP) of the Sun are on the same meridian. This means that the navigational triangle collapses into a straight line, and it can be solved by simple addition or subtraction. All we need is declination and the true sextant altitude. No Tables are needed and it is the time-hallowed and simplest way to monitor an ocean passage, or get a local noon latitude position line on any offshore trip. It has limitations – some obvious and some not!

Consider Fig 36 showing the yacht's meridian on the right of the circle, representing an elevation of the Earth, with poles top and bottom. At the time of the noon sight, when the Sun is at its highest

A

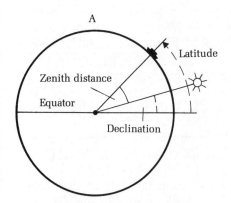

B

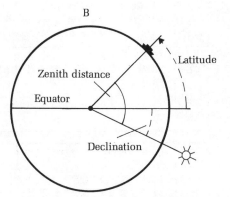

Latitude and declination both north.
'Same Name' so noon latitude equals
zenith distance *plus* declination

Latitude north, declination south.
'Opposite Names' so noon latitude
equals zenith distance *minus* declination.

Note: With any combination of latitude and declination:
'Same Name' add, 'Opposite Name' subtract.

*Fig 36   Noon sight – Lat/Dec. Opposite – Same Name. The yacht and the
GP of Sun are on the same line of meridian. The zenith distance is the
angular distance from the yacht to the GP of the Sun (calculated by
deducting the true sextant altitude from 90°). The declination is the angular
distance of the GP of the Sun north or south of the equator, at the time of the
noon sight. (From* Reed's Almanac.*)*

point, we can abstract the declination from *Reed's Almanac* which
is the geographical position north of the equator. This is effectively
its latitude and we regard it as that. We know that the sextant
measures the zenith distance, the angular distance from the above
geographical position to the yacht. So we simply add the zenith
distance to the declination, and that is our latitude. This is the case
in northern latitudes with north declination as shown. You might
be reminded here that we use sextant altitude for routine sight
reduction and zenith distance is 90° minus altitude. So noon
latitude is zenith distance plus or minus declination. Fig 36 shows
that with south declination and the yacht in north latitude, the

CONVERTING ARC INTO TIME & VICE-VERSA

Secs. (& decimals) of Arc into Secs. of Time

"	'	s
0 = 0·0		0·00
1		0·07
2		0·13
3		0·20
4		0·27
5		0·33
6 = 0·1		0·40
7		0·47
8		0·53
9		0·60
10		0·67
11		0·73
12 = 0·2		0·80
13		0·87
14		0·93
15		1·00
16		1·07
17		1·13
18 = 0·3		1·20
19		1·27
20		1·33
21		1·40
22		1·47
23		1·53
24 = 0·4		1·60
25		1·67
26		1·73
27		1·80
28		1·87
29		1·93
30 = 0·5		2·00

Mins. of Arc into Mins. and Secs. of Time

'	min.	s
0	0	0
1	0	4
2	0	8
3	0	12
4	0	16
5	0	20
6	0	24
7	0	28
8	0	32
9	0	36
10	0	40
11	0	44
12	0	48
13	0	52
14	0	56
15	1	0
16	1	4
17	1	8
18	1	12
19	1	16
20	1	20
21	1	24
22	1	28
23	1	32
24	1	36
25	1	40
26	1	44
27	1	48
28	1	52
29	1	56
30	2	0

DEGREES OF ARC INTO HOURS AND MINUTES.

°	h.min	°	h.min	°	h.min	°	h.min	°	h.min	°	h.min
0	0 0	60	4 0	120	8 0	180	12 0	240	16 0	300	20 0
1	0 4	61	4 4	121	8 4	181	12 4	241	16 4	301	20 4
2	0 8	62	4 8	122	8 8	182	12 8	242	16 8	302	20 8
3	0 12	63	4 12	123	8 12	183	12 12	243	16 12	303	20 12
4	0 16	64	4 16	124	8 16	184	12 16	244	16 16	304	20 16
5	0 20	65	4 20	125	8 20	185	12 20	245	16 20	305	20 20
6	0 24	66	4 24	126	8 24	186	12 24	246	16 24	306	20 24
7	0 28	67	4 28	127	8 28	187	12 28	247	16 28	307	20 28
8	0 32	68	4 32	128	8 32	188	12 32	248	16 32	308	20 32
9	0 36	69	4 36	129	8 36	189	12 36	249	16 36	309	20 36
10	0 40	70	4 40	130	8 40	190	12 40	250	16 40	310	20 40
11	0 44	71	4 44	131	8 44	191	12 44	251	16 44	311	20 44
12	0 48	72	4 48	132	8 48	192	12 48	252	16 48	312	20 48
13	0 52	73	4 52	133	8 52	193	12 52	253	16 52	313	20 52
14	0 56	74	4 56	134	8 56	194	12 56	254	16 56	314	20 56
15	1 0	75	5 0	135	9 0	195	13 0	255	17 0	315	21 0
16	1 4	76	5 4	136	9 4	196	13 4	256	17 4	316	21 4
17	1 8	77	5 8	137	9 8	197	13 8	257	17 8	317	21 8
18	1 12	78	5 12	138	9 12	198	13 12	258	17 12	318	21 12
19	1 16	79	5 16	139	9 16	199	13 16	259	17 16	319	21 16
20	1 20	80	5 20	140	9 20	200	13 20	260	17 20	320	21 20
21	1 24	81	5 24	141	9 24	201	13 24	261	17 24	321	21 24
22	1 28	82	5 28	142	9 28	202	13 28	262	17 28	322	21 28
23	1 32	83	5 32	143	9 32	203	13 32	263	17 32	323	21 32
24	1 36	84	5 36	144	9 36	204	13 36	264	17 36	324	21 36
25	1 40	85	5 40	145	9 40	205	13 40	265	17 40	325	21 40
26	1 44	86	5 44	146	9 44	206	13 44	266	17 44	326	21 44
27	1 48	87	5 48	147	9 48	207	13 48	267	17 48	327	21 48
28	1 52	88	5 52	148	9 52	208	13 52	268	17 52	328	21 52
29	1 56	89	5 56	149	9 56	209	13 56	269	17 56	329	21 56
30	2 0	90	6 0	150	10 0	210	14 0	270	18 0	330	22 0

Fig 37   Reed's Almanac 4:2

zenith distance traverses the equator to measure the angular distance from the yacht to the geographical position of the Sun, so we obviously *subtract* the declination to get the latitude.

A simple rule to remember is:

Declination and latitude (Same Name) – *add*
Different Name – *subtract*. (Name is north or south.)

Poole to Cherbourg, 3 March 1991
Timing the Noon Sight

In principle you are taking a sight at the Sun's highest altitude on the day. You can time it near enough and then allow a margin. Page 4:2 in *Reed's Almanac* (Fig 37) gives a Table to convert arc into time so your DR longitude will guide you from Greenwich noon. However, remember that the true Sun does not transit Greenwich at 12.00h exactly, the difference being known as the equation of time.

Take a practical example. On a simple cross-Channel passage, such as Poole to Cherbourg (Fig 38), you are often mid-Channel at

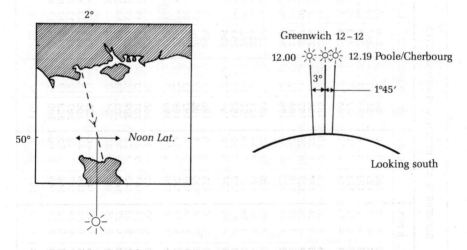

Fig 38   *Passage – Poole to Cherbourg – Sunday 3 March 1991.*
   Anvil Point abeam about 06.00. Speed made good about 5 knots. Greenwich hour angle at 12.00 is 357° (Reed's Almanac 3:24, Fig 39) so the Sun is about 3° late. At 4 mins/degree this is 12 minutes of time. Poole/Cherbourg meridian long. is about 1°45′ west – another 7 minutes – so transit will be about 12 hours 19 minutes. Roughly, the sextant altitude will be about 33°. The zenith distance is 57°.
   Declination is about 6°54′ south – decreasing. (Reed's Almanac 3:24, Fig 39.) Dec. and Lat. Opposite Name, so subtract – 57° minus 7° equals 50° north Lat. Cherbourg is 49°40′ so about 20 miles to go. ETA about 16.30 GMT.

Friday, 1st March

h	SUN G.H.A.	Dec.	ARIES G.H.A.	h
00	176 52.0	S 7 51.6	158 18.1	00
02	206 52.2	7 49.7	188 23.1	02
04	236 52.4	7 47.8	218 28.0	04
06	266 52.7	7 45.9	248 32.9	06
08	296 52.9	7 44.0	278 37.8	08
10	326 53.2	7 42.1	308 42.8	10
12	356 53.4	7 40.2	338 47.7	12
14	26 53.6	7 38.3	8 52.6	14
16	56 53.9	7 36.4	38 57.6	16
18	86 54.1	7 34.5	69 02.5	18
20	116 54.4	7 32.6	99 07.4	20
22	146 54.6	S 7 30.7	129 12.3	22

Saturday, 2nd March

h	SUN G.H.A.	Dec.	ARIES G.H.A.	h
00	176 54.9	S 7 28.8	159 17.3	00
02	206 55.1	7 26.9	189 22.2	02
04	236 55.4	7 25.0	219 27.1	04
06	266 55.6	7 23.1	249 32.1	06
08	296 55.9	7 21.2	279 37.0	08
10	326 56.1	7 19.3	309 41.9	10
12	356 56.4	7 17.4	339 46.8	12
14	26 56.6	7 15.5	9 51.8	14
16	56 56.9	7 13.5	39 56.7	16
18	86 57.1	7 11.6	70 01.6	18
20	116 57.4	7 09.7	100 06.5	20
22	146 57.6	S 7 07.8	130 11.5	22

Sunday, 3rd March

h	SUN G.H.A.	Dec.	ARIES G.H.A.	h
00	176 57.9	S 7 05.9	160 16.4	00
02	206 58.2	7 04.0	190 21.3	02
04	236 58.4	7 02.1	220 26.3	04
06	266 58.7	7 00.2	250 31.2	06
08	296 58.9	6 58.3	280 36.1	08
10	326 59.2	6 56.3	310 41.0	10
12	356 59.5	6 54.4	340 46.0	12
14	26 59.7	6 52.5	10 50.9	14
16	57 00.0	6 50.6	40 55.8	16
18	87 00.2	6 48.7	71 00.8	18
20	117 00.5	6 46.8	101 05.7	20
22	147 00.8	S 6 44.8	131 10.6	22

Monday, 4th March

h	SUN G.H.A.	Dec.	ARIES G.H.A.	h
00	177 01.0	S 6 42.9	161 15.5	00
02	207 01.3	6 41.0	191 20.5	02
04	237 01.6	6 39.1	221 25.4	04
06	267 01.9	6 37.2	251 30.3	06
08	297 02.1	6 35.3	281 35.3	08
10	327 02.4	6 33.3	311 40.2	10
12	357 02.7	6 31.4	341 45.1	12
14	27 02.9	6 29.5	11 50.0	14
16	57 03.2	6 27.6	41 55.0	16
18	87 03.5	6 25.6	71 59.9	18
20	117 03.8	6 23.7	102 04.8	20
22	147 04.0	S 6 21.8	132 09.8	22

Tuesday, 5th March

h	SUN G.H.A.	Dec.	ARIES G.H.A.	h
00	177 04.3	S 6 19.9	162 14.7	00
02	207 04.6	6 17.9	192 19.6	02
04	237 04.9	6 16.0	222 24.5	04
06	267 05.1	6 14.1	252 29.5	06
08	297 05.4	6 12.2	282 34.4	08
10	327 05.7	6 10.2	312 39.3	10
12	357 06.0	6 08.3	342 44.3	12
14	27 06.3	6 06.4	12 49.2	14
16	57 06.6	6 04.4	42 54.1	16
18	87 06.8	6 02.5	72 59.0	18
20	117 07.1	6 00.6	103 04.0	20
22	147 07.4	S 5 58.6	133 08.9	22

Wednesday, 6th March

h	SUN G.H.A.	Dec.	ARIES G.H.A.	h
00	177 07.7	S 5 56.7	163 13.8	00
02	207 08.0	5 54.8	193 18.8	02
04	237 08.3	5 52.8	223 23.7	04
06	267 08.5	5 50.9	253 28.6	06
08	297 08.8	5 49.0	283 33.5	08
10	327 09.1	5 47.0	313 38.5	10
12	357 09.4	5 45.1	343 43.4	12
14	27 09.7	5 43.2	13 48.3	14
16	57 10.0	5 41.2	43 53.2	16
18	87 10.3	5 39.3	73 58.2	18
20	117 10.6	5 37.3	104 03.1	20
22	147 10.9	S 5 35.4	134 08.0	22

Thursday, 7th March

h	SUN G.H.A.	Dec.	ARIES G.H.A.	h
00	177 11.2	S 5 33.5	164 13.0	00
02	207 11.5	5 31.5	194 17.9	02
04	237 11.8	5 29.6	224 22.8	04
06	267 12.1	5 27.6	254 27.7	06
08	297 12.3	5 25.7	284 32.7	08
10	327 12.6	5 23.8	314 37.6	10
12	357 12.9	5 21.8	344 42.5	12
14	27 13.2	5 19.9	14 47.5	14
16	57 13.5	5 17.9	44 52.4	16
18	87 13.8	5 16.0	74 57.3	18
20	117 14.1	5 14.0	105 02.2	20
22	147 14.4	S 5 12.1	135 07.2	22

Friday, 8th March

h	SUN G.H.A.	Dec.	ARIES G.H.A.	h
00	177 14.7	S 5 10.1	165 12.1	00
02	207 15.0	5 08.2	195 17.0	02
04	237 15.3	5 06.3	225 22.0	04
06	267 15.7	5 04.3	255 26.9	06
08	297 16.0	5 02.4	285 31.8	08
10	327 16.3	5 00.4	315 36.7	10
12	357 16.6	4 58.5	345 41.7	12
14	27 16.9	4 56.5	15 46.6	14
16	57 17.2	4 54.6	45 51.5	16
18	87 17.5	4 52.6	75 56.5	18
20	117 17.8	4 50.7	106 01.4	20
22	147 18.1	S 4 48.7	136 06.3	22

Saturday, 9th March

h	SUN G.H.A.	Dec.	ARIES G.H.A.	h
00	177 18.4	S 4 46.8	166 11.2	00
02	207 18.7	4 44.8	196 16.2	02
04	237 19.0	4 42.9	226 21.1	04
06	267 19.3	4 40.9	256 26.0	06
08	297 19.7	4 39.0	286 31.0	08
10	327 20.0	4 37.0	316 35.9	10
12	357 20.3	4 35.0	346 40.8	12
14	27 20.6	4 33.1	16 45.7	14
16	57 20.9	4 31.1	46 50.7	16
18	87 21.2	4 29.2	76 55.6	18
20	117 21.5	4 27.2	107 00.5	20
22	147 21.8	S 4 25.3	137 05.4	22

Sunday, 10th March

h	SUN G.H.A.	Dec.	ARIES G.H.A.	h
00	177 22.2	S 4 23.3	167 10.4	00
02	207 22.5	4 21.4	197 15.3	02
04	237 22.8	4 19.4	227 20.2	04
06	267 23.1	4 17.4	257 25.2	06
08	297 23.4	4 15.5	287 30.1	08
10	327 23.7	4 13.5	317 35.0	10
12	357 24.1	4 11.6	347 39.9	12
14	27 24.4	4 09.6	17 44.9	14
16	57 24.7	4 07.7	47 49.8	16
18	87 25.0	4 05.7	77 54.7	18
20	117 25.4	4 03.7	107 59.7	20
22	147 25.7	S 4 01.8	138 04.6	22

Monday, 11th March

h	SUN G.H.A.	Dec.	ARIES G.H.A.	h
00	177 26.0	S 3 59.8	168 09.5	00
02	207 26.3	3 57.9	198 14.4	02
04	237 26.6	3 55.9	228 19.4	04
06	267 27.0	3 53.9	258 24.3	06
08	297 27.3	3 52.0	288 29.2	08
10	327 27.6	3 50.0	318 34.2	10
12	357 27.9	3 48.0	348 39.1	12
14	27 28.3	3 46.1	18 44.0	14
16	57 28.6	3 44.1	48 48.9	16
18	87 28.9	3 42.1	78 53.9	18
20	117 29.2	3 40.2	108 58.8	20
22	147 29.6	S 3 38.2	139 03.7	22

Tuesday, 12th March

h	SUN G.H.A.	Dec.	ARIES G.H.A.	h
00	177 29.9	S 3 36.3	169 08.7	00
02	207 30.2	3 34.3	199 13.6	02
04	237 30.6	3 32.3	229 18.5	04
06	267 30.9	3 30.4	259 23.4	06
08	297 31.2	3 28.4	289 28.4	08
10	327 31.6	3 26.4	319 33.3	10
12	357 31.9	3 24.5	349 38.2	12
14	27 32.2	3 22.5	19 43.2	14
16	57 32.6	3 20.5	49 48.1	16
18	87 32.9	3 18.6	79 53.0	18
20	117 33.2	3 16.6	109 57.9	20
22	147 33.6	S 3 14.6	140 02.9	22

Wednesday, 13th March

h	SUN G.H.A.	Dec.	ARIES G.H.A.	h
00	177 33.9	S 3 12.7	170 07.8	00
02	207 34.2	3 10.7	200 12.7	02
04	237 34.6	3 08.7	230 17.7	04
06	267 34.9	3 06.7	260 22.6	06
08	297 35.2	3 04.8	290 27.5	08
10	327 35.6	3 02.8	320 32.4	10
12	357 35.9	3 00.8	350 37.4	12
14	27 36.2	2 58.9	20 42.3	14
16	57 36.6	2 56.9	50 47.2	16
18	87 36.9	2 54.9	80 52.1	18
20	117 37.3	2 53.0	110 57.1	20
22	147 37.6	S 2 51.0	141 02.0	22

Thursday, 14th March

h	SUN G.H.A.	Dec.	ARIES G.H.A.	h
00	177 37.9	S 2 49.0	171 06.9	00
02	207 38.3	2 47.0	201 11.9	02
04	237 38.6	2 45.1	231 16.8	04
06	267 39.0	2 43.1	261 21.7	06
08	297 39.3	2 41.1	291 26.6	08
10	327 39.6	2 39.2	321 31.6	10
12	357 40.0	2 37.2	351 36.5	12
14	27 40.3	2 35.2	21 41.4	14
16	57 40.7	2 33.2	51 46.4	16
18	87 41.0	2 31.3	81 51.3	18
20	117 41.4	2 29.3	111 56.2	20
22	147 41.7	S 2 27.3	142 01.1	22

Friday, 15th March

h	SUN G.H.A.	Dec.	ARIES G.H.A.	h
00	177 42.1	S 2 25.3	172 06.1	00
02	207 42.4	2 23.4	202 11.0	02
04	237 42.7	2 21.4	232 15.9	04
06	267 43.1	2 19.4	262 20.9	06
08	297 43.4	2 17.4	292 25.8	08
10	327 43.8	2 15.5	322 30.7	10
12	357 44.1	2 13.5	352 35.6	12
14	27 44.5	2 11.5	22 40.6	14
16	57 44.8	2 09.5	52 45.5	16
18	87 45.2	2 07.6	82 50.4	18
20	117 45.5	2 05.6	112 55.4	20
22	147 45.9	S 2 03.6	143 00.3	22

To interpolate **SUN** G.H.A. see page 4:7   To interpolate **ARIES** G.H.A. see page 4:8

Fig 39   Reed's Almanac *3:24*

local noon. This is ideal for a noon latitude because it tells you what remains of the 60-mile trip. You should know your Speed Made Good (SMG) by then and give the skipper a reasonable estimated time of arrival (ETA).

To embrace the maximum number of the above points, take such a trip on Sunday 3 March, you in north latitude and the Sun in south declination. The Greenwich hour angle (GHA) at noon is 357° – *see Reed's Almanac* 3:24 (Fig 39). So the Sun is 360° – 357° late – 3 degrees – each worth 4 minutes of time so that is 12 minutes late – *see Reed's Almanac* 4:2 (Fig 37). But Poole is west of Greenwich by about 1°45′ so that is another 7 minutes, giving a total of 19 minutes past 12.00h for your noon sight. What numbers are you likely to get? (Latitude equals zenith distance minus declination.) Declination will be about 7° south – *see Reed's Almanac* 3:24 (Fig 39). Be accurate on the day. Latitude is going to be about 50°N., the sextant altitude about 33°; 90° minus 33° equals 57°, minus 7° equals 50° latitude. About right!

Conclusions on Noon Sights

Remember they flourished when we had no accurate time or Tables. So it is O.K. if you have no Tables aboard. I find waiting for the Sun to reach its highest point after allowing a time margin is tedious, and a passing cloud can obscure it. You must understand noon sights, but a straightforward sight can be quicker and less frustrating. The RYA 'Ocean' requires a Sun-Run-Sun which normally includes a noon latitude.

Sun Sights Review

Equipment required: sextant; watch; protractor; dividers; hand bearing-compass (Fig 40).
Publications: *Reed's Almanac*; *Sight Reduction Tables* (A.P. 3270) – Volume 2 for latitudes 0° to 39°, Volume 3 for latitudes 40° to 89°; a suitable chart or plotting sheet; Flowchart B from this book (see Fig 2 on page 12).

Definitions

'Away/Towards' The direction to move the intercept along the azimuth from the chosen position – 'towards' if the sextant angle is greater, and vice versa.

THE SUN SIGHT

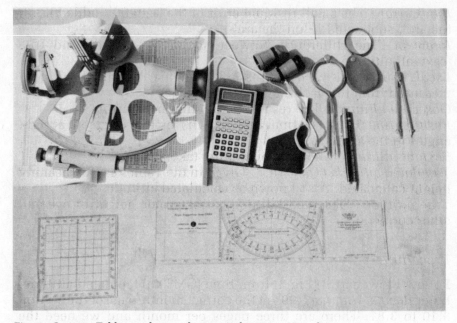

Fig 40   Sextant, Tables, and some chart-room furniture. Note the 5 × 25 monocular (Russian), the ubiquitous 'Duggie' protractor, and the Jean Cras rapporteur, beloved of the French.

Azimuth   The bearing of the body at time of sight, given in the Tables. (Check with the hand bearing-compass.)

Chosen latitude   Your DR latitude rounded to the nearest whole degree.

Chosen longitude   Your DR longitude rounded to the nearest whole degree of LHA. To obtain from the GHA, subtract west longitude and add east longitude.

Chosen position (CP)   The combination of chosen latitude/longitude. The first plot on the chart.

Dead reckoning (DR) position   Your best estimate of your position in latitude/longitude at the time of sight.

Declination (Dec.)   Effectively, the celestial latitude of the body. The Sun is recorded as moving from 23½° north in summer to the same position south in winter.

GOAT   Greater Observed Angle Towards.

Greenwich hour angle (GHA)   The angular distance measured westwards, up to 360°, of the point directly under the Sun (its geographical position or GP) from the Greenwich meridian, at the time of sight.

Index error   The small residual error of the sextant – added if 'off the arc', subtracted if 'on the arc'.

Intercept   The difference between tabulated altitude and true (sextant) altitude.

Local hour angle (LHA)   A similar angular distance to GHA, measured from the yacht to the Sun's GP.

Observed altitude   The result of applying index error.

Position line (PL)   The final line, drawn from the intercept at right angles to the azimuth.

Sextant altitude   The sextant reading taken.

Tabulated altitude (Tab. Alt.)   Given in the Tables as Hc, meaning height calculated. Also known as calculated altitude.

True altitude   Observed altitude corrected for height of eye and other corrections.

Procedure

Follow Flowchart B (Fig 2) from time (GMT) to tabulated altitude. Enter *Reed's Almanac* 1991 at the correct month/page of the section 3.10 to 3.81. There are three pages per month and we need the middle pages giving Sun and Aries. Note GHA for the nearest two hours, lower value, and note the declination, estimating the value for the actual time.

Now turn to 4:7 (Fig 13) and apply the increments of time values from the two-hour figure to the actual time, giving GHA.

Now subtract west longitude; add east longitude to the GHA to lose the minutes, giving a whole number of LHA. For west longitude, apply the same minutes of longitude as the GHA and the degree which gives the nearest to DR. Subtracting loses the minutes. For east longitude, subtract the GHA minutes from 60 and make this your chosen longitude, adjusting the degree as before.

Now enter the Tables with latitude (nearest whole degree) plus declination and LHA. Find the group of pages with the required latitude and identify 'Same' or 'Contrary Name'. This means declination and latitude, north/south. Abstract Hc, *d* and Z.

Use Table 5 (Fig 18) to correct Hc for the minutes of declination, noting the sign. Take the *d* value along the top horizontal line. Come down to the minutes you have to account for and apply the given correction to Hc.

You now have the tabulated altitude. Read off Z and check the head- and footnotes to see if it needs modifying to give Zn. The hand bearing-compass reading you took will be a check.

Now to correct the sextant reading. Apply the index error,

G.M.T.   (31 days)   G.M.T.

☉ SUN ☉

Yr.	Mth.	Week	Equation of Time 0 h.	12 h.	Transit	Semi-diam.	Lat. 52 N. Twilight	Sun-rise	Sun-set	Twilight	Lat.	Lat. Corr. Twilight	Sun-rise	Sun-set	Twilight
			m. s.	m. s.	h. m.	'	h. m.	h. m.	h. m.	h. m.		h. m.	h. m.	h. m.	h. m.
60	1	Fri.	+12 32	+12 27	12 12	16.2	06 13	06 47	17 39	18 13	N70	-0 18	+0 08	-0 06	+0 19
61	2	Sat.	+12 21	+12 15	12 12	16.2	06 11	06 45	17 40	18 14	68	-0 15	+0 06	-0 05	+0 15
62	3	Sun.	+12 09	+12 02	12 12	16.2	06 09	06 43	17 42	18 16	66	-0 12	+0 05	-0 04	+0 13
63	4	Mon.	+11 56	+11 50	12 12	16.2	06 07	06 41	17 44	18 18	64	-0 09	+0 04	-0 03	+0 10
64	5	Tu.	+11 43	+11 36	12 12	16.1	06 04	06 38	17 46	18 19	62	-0 06	+0 03	-0 02	+0 07
65	6	Wed.	+11 30	+11 23	12 11	16.1	06 02	06 36	17 48	18 21	N60	-0 04	+0 03	-0 02	+0 05
66	7	Th.	+11 16	+11 09	12 11	16.1	06 00	06 34	17 50	18 23	58	-0 03	+0 02	-0 02	+0 04
67	8	Fri.	+11 01	+10 54	12 11	16.1	05 58	06 31	17 51	18 25	56	-0 01	+0 01	-0 01	+0 02
68	9	Sat.	+10 47	+10 39	12 11	16.1	05 56	06 29	17 53	18 27	54	0 01	+0 01	-0 01	+0 01
69	10	Sun.	+10 32	+10 24	12 10	16.1	05 54	06 27	17 55	18 29	50	+0 01	0 00	0 00	-0 01
70	11	Mon.	+10 16	+10 09	12 10	16.1	05 51	06 24	17 56	18 30	N45	+0 03	-0 01	+0 02	-0 02
71	12	Tu.	+10 01	+09 53	12 10	16.1	05 49	06 22	17 58	18 32	40	+0 05	-0 02	+0 02	-0 04
72	13	Wed.	+09 45	+09 37	12 10	16.1	05 47	06 20	18 00	18 34	35	+0 06	-0 03	+0 03	-0 05
73	14	Th.	+09 29	+09 21	12 09	16.1	05 44	06 18	18 02	18 35	30	+0 07	0 04	+0 04	-0 06
74	15	Fri.	+09 12	+09 04	12 09	16.1	05 42	06 16	18 04	18 37	20	+0 07	0 05	+0 05	-0 06
75	16	Sat.	+08 55	+08 47	12 09	16.1	05 40	06 14	18 06	18 39	N10	+0 07	0 07	+0 06	-0 06
76	17	Sun.	+08 39	+08 30	12 08	16.1	05 37	06 11	18 07	18 40	0	+0 06	-0 08	+0 07	0 05
77	18	Mon.	+08 21	+08 13	12 08	16.1	05 35	06 09	18 09	18 42	S10	+0 04	-0 09	+0 09	-0 03
78	19	Tu.	+08 04	+07 55	12 08	16.1	05 33	06 07	18 11	18 44	20	+0 01	-0 11	+0 10	0 00
79	20	Wed.	+07 46	+07 38	12 08	16.1	05 30	06 04	18 12	18 46	30	-0 03	-0 14	+0 12	+0 04
80	21	Th.	+07 29	+07 20	12 07	16.1	05 28	06 02	18 14	18 48	S35	-0 06	-0 15	+0 14	+0 07
81	22	Fri.	+07 11	+07 02	12 07	16.1	05 26	06 00	18 15	18 50	40	-0 10	-0 17	+0 15	+0 11
82	23	Sat.	+06 53	+06 44	12 07	16.1	05 23	05 57	18 17	18 51	45	-0 13	0 18	+0 17	+0 14
83	24	Sun.	+06 35	+06 26	12 06	16.1	05 21	05 55	18 19	18 53	S50	-0 18	-0 20	+0 19	+0 20
84	25	Mon.	+06 17	+06 08	12 06	16.1	05 19	05 53	18 21	18 55					
85	26	Tu.	+05 59	+05 49	12 06	16.1	05 16	05 50	18 22	18 56					
86	27	Wed.	+05 40	+05 31	12 06	16.1	05 14	05 48	18 24	18 58					
87	28	Th.	+05 22	+05 13	12 05	16.1	05 12	05 46	18 26	19 00					
88	29	Fri.	+05 04	+04 55	12 05	16.0	05 09	05 43	18 27	19 02					
89	30	Sat.	+04 46	+04 37	12 05	16.0	05 07	05 41	18 29	19 04					
90	31	Sun.	+04 27	+04 18	12 04	16.0	05 05	05 39	18 31	19 06					

NOTES

The Lat. corr. to sunrise, etc., is for the middle of March. Examples of how to use the above data are given on page 2:11 onwards.

Equation of Time is the excess of Mean Time over Apparent Time (See explanation and examples on p. 2:15)

☾ MOON ☽

Yr.	Mth.	Week	Age days	Transit Diff. (Upper)	Semi-diam.	Hor. Par. 12 h.	Lat. 52 N. Moonrise	Moonset
				h. m. m.	'		h. m.	h. m.
60	1	Fri.	15	00 19 46	15.8	58.1	19 03	06 38
61	2	Sat.	16	01 05 46	15.6	57.4	20 21	06 53
62	3	Sun.	17	01 51 46	15.4	56.6	21 39	07 08
63	4	Mon.	18	02 37 47	15.2	55.9	22 55	07 24
64	5	Tu.	19	03 24 48	15.1	55.3	– –	07 44
65	6	Wed.	20	04 12 49	14.9	54.8	00 08	08 09
66	7	Th.	21	05 01 51	14.8	54.4	01 17	08 41
67	8	Fri.	22	05 52 50	14.8	54.3	02 19	09 23
68	9	Sat.	23	06 42 50	14.8	54.3	03 11	10 15
69	10	Sun.	24	07 32 49	14.8	54.4	03 51	11 17
70	11	Mon.	25	08 21 47	14.9	54.7	04 22	12 26
71	12	Tu.	26	09 08 46	15.0	55.2	04 47	13 39
72	13	Wed.	27	09 54 45	15.2	55.8	05 06	14 54
73	14	Th.	28	10 39 45	15.4	56.4	05 22	16 10
74	15	Fri.	29	11 24 45	15.5	57.0	05 37	17 26
75	16	Sat.	00	12 09 47	15.7	57.6	05 51	18 45
76	17	Sun.	01	12 56 50	15.8	58.2	06 06	20 06
77	18	Mon.	02	13 46 53	16.0	58.6	06 23	21 30
78	19	Tu.	03	14 39 57	16.1	58.9	06 44	22 55
79	20	Wed.	04	15 36 60	16.1	59.1	07 12	– –
80	21	Th.	05	16 36 62	16.1	59.3	07 50	00 17
81	22	Fri.	06	17 38 61	16.2	59.3	08 43	01 31
82	23	Sat.	07	18 39 58	16.1	59.1	09 51	02 30
83	24	Sun.	08	19 37 55	16.1	59.0	11 10	03 14
84	25	Mon.	09	20 32 51	16.0	58.9	12 34	03 46
85	26	Tu.	10	21 23 48	16.0	58.6	13 58	04 10
86	27	Wed.	11	22 11 46	15.9	58.2	15 20	04 28
87	28	Th.	12	22 57 46	15.7	57.8	16 40	04 44
88	29	Fri.	13	23 43 46	15.6	57.3	17 59	04 59
89	30	Sat.	14	24 29 46	15.5	56.7	19 16	05 13
90	31	Sun.	15	00 29 46	15.3	56.1	20 33	05 29

MOON'S PHASES

		d.	h.	m.
☾	Last Quarter	8	10	32
●	New Moon	16	08	10
☽	First Quarter...........	23	06	03
○	Full Moon	30	07	17

	d.	h.
Apogee	9	01
Perigee	22	05

NOTES

Moon's G.H.A. and Dec. are given on page 3:27.

A table for correcting Moonrise and Moonset for latitude is on page 4:20.

A table for correcting Moon's meridian passage for longitude is on page 4:19.

Examples on the use of the above data are given on page 2:11 onwards.

0h. = midnight. For explanation of use of above data see page 2:11 onwards.

Fig 41   Reed's Almanac 3:22.

checking it by viewing the direct and reflected horizon lines and noting the difference from zero on the micrometer scale.

Now enter 4:5 (Fig 14) in *Reed's Almanac* with observed altitude and height of eye, coming out with the correction to be added. You now have true altitude.

Now we can plot the position line. Enter the chosen position on the chart. Through this draw the azimuth. Compare true altitude with tabulated altitude as shown on Flowchart A (Fig 1) and decide 'Towards' or 'Away'. If your true altitude is greater you were obviously nearer the Sun, so this is 'Towards', and vice versa. With your dividers step off the intercept along the azimuth (each minute equals a nautical mile), and then draw the position line at right angles to the azimuth.

Decide how you are going to use this position line. You can take another sight in, say, three hours' time to cross the position lines at a reasonable angle and do a running fix, that is, plot your course and distance run from first fix and move this up to cross the second line. Quite a sensible ploy is to move your DR the shortest distance to the position line, thus giving a Most Probable Position (MPP). In all cases, log the course steered and the distance log reading at the time of sight.

Noon Sight for Latitude

Check the index error carefully. Obtain a sextant reading with the Sun at the highest altitude. Abstract declination from *Reed's Almanac*. The latitude is (90° minus true altitude) plus or minus declination. Plus if 'Same Name' (north/south), minus if 'Opposite Name'.

For timing: apply DR longitude in time from Greenwich noon, applying equation of time. It is easiest to take this from the Sun transit. An example is *Reed's Almanac* 3:22 (Fig 41) 3 March 1991 – sun transit 12h 12min.

Summary of Part One

After a brief historical preamble, Part One provides complete coverage of the planning, shooting, and plotting of the classic celestial navigation Sun shot; and the follow-up procedures required to record a daily position on an ocean passage.

There are many worked examples, all supported by relevant publications extracts, so that the reader may verify and check the calculations without invoking external sources.

THE SUN SIGHT

The flowcharts allow the event points to be identified and followed sequentially. Readers with some knowledge can quickly skip through these sequences but dwell on any points which trouble them. Very thorough analysis is accorded to recognized learning problems.

Part Two: Consolidation

This section sets out to fill in some of the topics deliberately left in the 'notional' stage in Part One. There is no flowchart to plough through and the topics can be picked up or skipped according to the reader's interest.

The PZX Triangle

This presents a problem in spherical trigonometry, and its solutions are elegant. These triangles have their sides, as well as their internal angles, measured in angular measure and they are all part of great circles, that is, their planes pass through the centre of the Earth. Fig 42 shows that the side from the pole to the yacht, PZ, is obviously

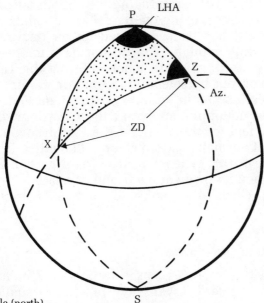

P = Elevated pole (north)
Z = Position of yacht
X = GP of Sun
LHA = Local hour angle*

Az. = Azimuth
ZD = Zenith distance
*LHA is same as difference in longitude (D'Long.)

Fig 42   The PZX triangle.

a great circle as it is on the yacht's meridian and its angular length is its co-latitude, that is, the distance from its declared latitude to the pole (90° minus latitude).

Similarly, the side PX from the pole to the geographical position of the Sun can have the Sun's declination treated as latitude and is its co-latitude or, more properly, its polar distance, which is the same thing. The remaining side, ZX, from the geographical position of the Sun, we already know to be the zenith distance, another great circle. The angle between the polar sides, PX and PZ is the local hour angle, which we know how to calculate.

In brief, we know enough to solve all six angles because only one triangle can satisfy all the above facts. So what do we need to know? Well, we need the azimuth so we can truly draw the required line from the chosen position. We also need the calculated zenith distance (expressed as altitude) to compare with the sextant altitude and so derive the intercept. You will now have realized that this is precisely what we get from the Tables. By feeding in our contributions as previously covered, we extract tabulated (calculated) altitude and azimuth.

The pre-computed Tables form one way of solving the PZX triangle, and they involve massaging the chosen latitude and LHA to form whole degrees, using the described methods of cancelling out the minutes. They were designed for air navigation and are quick and accurate enough. You do not have to specify whether your latitude is north or south when entering the Tables, as this problem is taken out by selecting 'Same' or 'Contrary' name for latitude and declination. In Volume 1 of the *Sight Reduction Tables* (stars) this does not apply, and you choose north or south latitude directly. Get a feel for the shape of the PZX triangle. The zenith distance cannot normally exceed about 5,000 miles. This implies a sextant altitude of 10°. When you stroll in the garden at twilight, is there a time when both you and a friend or relative in distant parts can see the Sun? Bristol in the UK to Perth in Australia? Bristol to Sydney?

Trigonometrical Solutions

This is a logarithmic process, used by Francis Chichester (in the air!) and once standard Royal Navy practice. Usually known as Haversine-Versine, they are just tricks to deal with negative numbers. With these you operate straight from the DR position (see *Reed's Almanac* 5:25) and go through the Versine Tables – but beware as it is easy to get lost.

Fig 43   *Interesting sky, somewhere near the Azores . . .*

Fig 44   *. . . leads to exhilarating sailing.*

CONSOLIDATION

Electronic Calculators

Programmable calculators, with built-in ephemerides, are beyond the scope of this book, but there is a very strong case in my view for the simple calculator as a back-up. *Reed's Almanac* covers this in 5:21. We can summarize.

Calculated altitude is covered as follows:

$$\text{Sin Alt.} = \text{Cos LHA} \times \text{Cos Lat.} \times \text{Cos Dec.} \pm \text{Sin Lat.} \times \text{Sin Dec.}$$

The minus sign is used if latitude and declination are different names (north/south). I suggest this for azimuth:

$$\text{Sin Az.} = \frac{\text{Sin LHA} \times \text{Cos Dec.}}{\text{Cos Alt.}}$$

Books will tell of Weir's Azimuth Diagram which looks well on coffee tables, and of the ABC Tables which *Reed's* say are quick and easy. However I have seen strong men distressed by them; do not attempt to learn them under pressure!

Calculators and Great Circles

We have seen that the global paths traced by the PZX triangle are great circles, and therefore the optimum routes for long ocean voyages are likely to be so also. This is certainly the case, but note that voyages due north or south are along Mercator meridians and therefore great circles.

Consider Fig 42 and imagine that the yacht is still at Z (say in the Western Approaches) but that the geographical position of the Sun at X is replaced by the latitude/longitude of a desired destination, say Bermuda. You are simply swapping a declination and hour angle for latitude/longitude. When you plot the azimuth you define this course but the chart or plotting sheet is on a Mercator projection, where the meridian PZ is vertical and the azimuth ZX is a simple angle from it. The message is that we cannot plot great circle courses from Mercator charts.

By regarding the position of Bermuda at the geographical position of a heavenly body, we can solve the PZX triangle as usual and come up with zenith distance and azimuth. So we have the great circle distance from the yacht to Bermuda and the initial great circle course. We simply have to convert the angular zenith distance to nautical miles by the exchange rate of 60 miles per

Fig 45   The weather settling down.

Fig 46   Sky clearing, but still hooked on.

CONSOLIDATION

Fig 47   Relaxed conditions – ideal for compass check by amplitude.

Fig 48   Re-establish position – Terry checks.

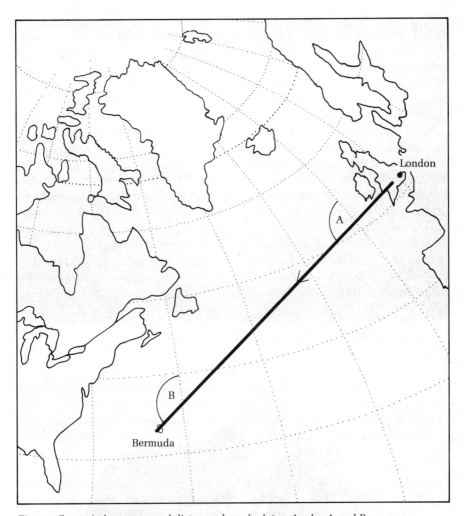

Fig 49   Great circle courses and distances by calculator. Angles A and B are different so the Mercator course would be unsuitable. You need a great circle solution so plot Lat./Long. as declination and LHA (difference of Long.), thus treating Bermuda as a body in geostationary orbit. From the yacht's DR, calculate the azimuth and zenith distance. This gives a great circle course and distance to go. Repeat every few days of the voyage.

degree. Fig 49 shows this situation as an atlas depicts it. There are other ways of getting great circle courses/distances, which are discussed later on, but the obvious one of doing the above calculation by the Tables is awkward because you are moving from latitude 50°N. to about latitude 32°N. which means changing from Volume 3 (39°–89°) to Volume 2 (0°–40°).

CONSOLIDATION

The calculator is wonderfully convenient in this application, using the simple trigonometrical formulae given above. Bermuda is your fixed destination. Regard it as the geographical position of a satellite in stationary orbit. So its declination (latitude) is fixed, and the local hour angle is simply the difference in longitude (D'long) between the meridian of Bermuda and the yacht's meridian. Fig 42 should make this clear.

Each day the yacht will have a different DR position (hopefully!). Perform the standard calculations, which will give you calculated altitude and azimuth. Subtract altitude from 90° to give the zenith distance and convert from arc to miles. This is your distance to go. Apply variation (and/or deviation) if appropriate to the azimuth and that is your course for the day, if you can fetch it. Repeat the exercise every few days or as appropriate, and revert to standard navigation when within 400–500 miles, when the difference between the two forms of navigation will be negligible. Magnetic variation on ocean charts is not shown on compass roses but by isogonals – lines of equal magnetic variation.

Chart Projections and Great Circle Courses

Fig 50 shows some ways of representing the spherical Earth on a flat chart, each solution involving a compromise somewhere. The Mercator projection which we mostly use has the advantage that course lines (called rhumb-lines) cross meridians at the same angle, but are not great circles.

The latitude scale increases north and south of the equator and distances have to be taken from the latitude scales adjacent to the point of interest. This projection does not work in polar regions as can be deduced from the example shown in Fig 50.

There is a transverse Mercator projection which we will bypass and come to the Gnomonic projection. Straight lines on this *are* great circles, and it has rather diverse uses. They range from coverage of polar regions to harbour plans and, of course, the generation of great circles courses. So we can generate required courses from Gnomonic charts and plot them as short courses on Mercator charts. We can further place a latitude limit to respect an icing hazard, for example, and this then becomes a composite course. There are also clever graphical and mathematical solutions to the great circle problem. Finally, remember that a great circle route, although the shortest over the ground, is not necessarily the best route. You need

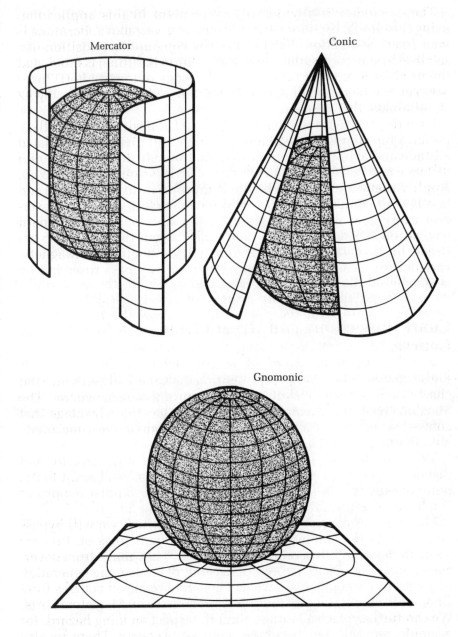

Fig 50   Examples of projecting latitude and longitude from the three-dimensional Earth on to a two-dimensional surface.

CONSOLIDATION

to study wind patterns, currents and so on which can be gleaned from Admiralty Routing Charts. These are issued for each month and are available from chart agents. The wind 'roses' give likely frequencies of wind strength and direction based on the number of recorded observations from that spot. Ocean currents are depicted and your courses should allow for these as you do for tidal streams in coastal navigation.

Chartwork Aids

We cannot escape the requirement to convert the various compass headings back and forth: TRUE – MAGNETIC – COMPASS.
There are several aphorisms and mnemonics, such as:

Tall	**V**irgins	**M**ake	**D**ull	**C**ompany
TRUE	**v**ariation	**MAGNETIC**	**d**eviation	**COMPASS**

If you found the flowcharts (Figs 1 and 2) useful, the same philosophy brought me to the 'Three Eggs' solution (Fig 51). You simply enter the figure with the given input, follow the flowpath and emerge with the required output. This is very popular with students, both on the water and in the classroom.

Another requirement, which is growing with electronic navigation outputs and waypoint inputs, is plotting latitude/longitude position. You might be doing your astro-navigation in parallel with such systems at times, and there are some clumsy practices involving Breton Plotters and so on, moving over vast chart distances.

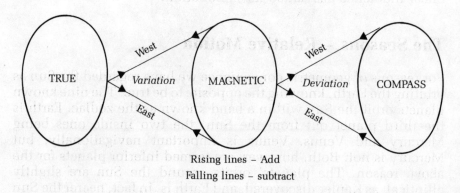

Fig 51   The 'Three Eggs'.

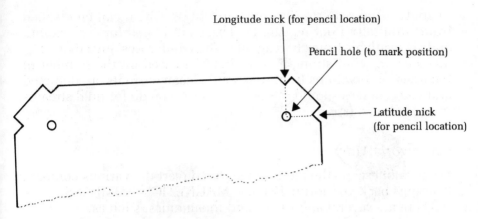

Fig 52 The 'Nadger'.

So I have developed the 'Nadger' – so called because it is indescribable!

Fig 52 shows the layout. It was designed backwards:

1. The final chart position to be marked by twiddling a pencil point in a small hole in the matt surface plastic device.
2. There must be a positive location for the pencil point when taking latitude/longitude co-ordinates from the chart.
3. Minimal movements from start to finish, in a standard sequence.
4. Must be a 'comfortable' and cheap addition to chart table furniture, with additional functions, for example recording bearings.

Sheer indolence has halted its exploitation!

The Seasons – Relative Motion

For reasons of geometric convenience we have regarded the Sun as orbiting the Earth, knowing the opposite to be true. The nine known planets orbit the Sun within a band known as the zodiac. Earth is the third planet out from the Sun, the two inside ones being Mercury and Venus. Venus is important navigationally, but Mercury is not. Both, however, are termed inferior planets for the above reason. The planets' orbits around the Sun are slightly elliptical, as Kepler discovered, and Earth is, in fact, nearer the Sun in our winter than in summer (*see* Fig 53.)

CONSOLIDATION

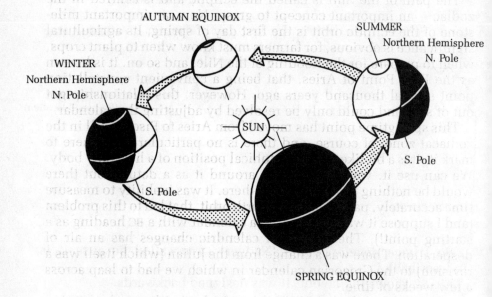

Fig 53   *The seasons.*

A complication of the Earth's errant nature, leading directly to the seasons, is the fact that its own spinning axis is inclined at 23½° to the path of its orbit around the Sun. Each pole is tilted towards the Sun at a definite time of its orbital cycle and away from the Sun six months later. At intermediate times the tilt is not 'to' and 'from' but sideways. Obviously, the tilt 'to' in the Northern Hemisphere gives our summers (longest days) notionally peaking on 21 June; and 'from' gives midwinter on 21 December (shortest days). The intermediate times, in March and September, where the sideways tilt has no effect on relative lengths of night and day, are the equinoctials – equal days and nights everywhere. The calendar times at which these phenomena occur are important for agricultural and religious events, and it would be a tragedy to get one of these wrongly timed.

These celestial movements are better understood if we revert to our previous notion of the Sun easing itself around the Earth, slowly spiralling between 23½° north and south of the terrestrial equator. The frame of reference for these movements has to be astrological and related to the fixed star constellations, with us confining ourselves to the zone of the zodiac.

The path of the Sun is called the ecliptic and is centred in the zodiac – an important concept to grasp. Now, an important milestone of the ecliptic orbit is the first day of spring. Its agricultural significance is obvious, for farmers must know when to plant crops, when to prepare for the flooding of the Nile, and so on. It is known as the First Point of Aries, that being a convenient constellation point several thousand years ago. However, this relationship got out of step and could only be resolved by adjusting the calendar.

This springtime point has moved from Aries to Pisces, still in the zodiacal zone, of course, and there is no particular body there to mark it. It is a bit like the geographical position of a heavenly body. We can use it, we can calculate around it as a datum, but there would be nothing to see if you got there. It was inability to measure time accurately, particularly the Earth orbit, that led to this problem (and I suppose it was hard to find a calendar with a BC heading as a starting point!). The history of calendric changes has an air of desperation. There was a change from the Julian (which itself was a revision) to the Gregorian calendar in which we had to leap across a few weeks of time.

In Part One we dealt with time in a fairly simple way by looking at just what we needed to work a Sun shot. To understand the treatment of other navigational bodies we need to probe further, and this is the next step.

Time

Some aspects of this fascinating subject are important for an understanding of navigational calculations. Others are interesting but not directly helpful, so its treatment tends to be subjective, as the dividing line is not rigid.

Solar Time

I have shown that the apparent path of the Sun, the ecliptic, is oblique to what we regard as the celestial equator – the equinoctial (*see* Fig 54). Further, the orbit of the Earth around the Sun is elliptical and the Earth is not at its centre. These two effects, obliquity and eccentricity, make the true Sun unsuitable for time-keeping – the Earth travels faster when nearer the Sun and vice versa, so minutes and seconds would not be regular. Instead, we invoke the concept of an imaginary mean Sun which behaves regularly, and regard every rotation of the Earth, meridian to same

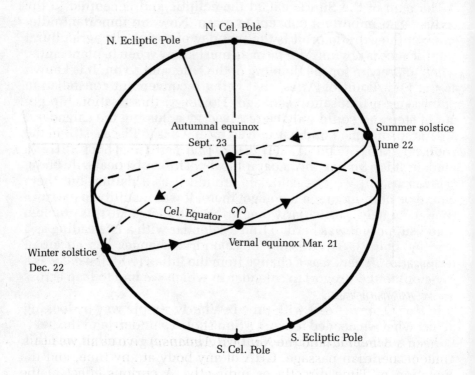

Fig 54   The ecliptic.

meridian, as a mean solar day of 24 hours.

This is fine for most of our activities but it is the true, or apparent Sun, we shoot with the sextant so, navigationally, we have to tangle with the exchange rate between these two times. We are equipped to deal with this problem, which is known as the Equation of Time (*see* Fig 55).

We need time in a calendar sense for declination, but most of our work is in hour angles, so we should become familiar with the expression Greenwich hour angle mean Sun and Greenwich hour angle true Sun. Fig 55 shows that the extreme differences are about plus/minus 15–20 minutes. The base line is mean Sun and the Equation of Time will be positive or negative on this. When we looked up Greenwich meridian passage for the noon sight, we saw that the true Sun could be early or late, although there are four times in the year when there is briefly no difference.

84

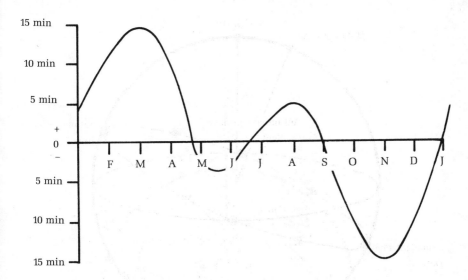

Fig 55 Equation of Time.

Reed's Almanac (and the *Nautical Almanac*) give us all we need: time of meridian passage, GHA of any body at any time, and the Equation of Time directly or indirectly. A curious effect of the Equation of Time, pointed out to me by an astute student, occurs around Christmas and the New Year. You would think, he said, that after the shortest day of 21 December, sunrise would be slightly earlier. In fact, it is not so, and we are into January before sunrise behaves as expected. The days, of course, do get longer. You will see that the curve is very steep at this time, and the Equation of Time changes its sign. You should have no problems if you now see why, when timing a noon sight, you apply the estimated difference of longitude in time to the time of the meridian passage.

Time is inseparably linked with longitude. Fig 56 shows the Sun over the Greenwich meridian at noon. Each radial mark is ¹/₂₄th of a circle, that is 15°, and indicates the centres of time zones. In a solar day of 24 hours, the Sun sweeps each zone in 1 hour. The zones are numbered and given a sign, plus or minus. Going east the sign is negative, and minus 2, for instance, indicates the zone 30° or 2 hours east of Greenwich. Note well that the numbers and signs show the correction to be applied to convert to GMT (or universal time (UT) as it is now often known).

French tide tables are in Zone 1. You have to knock off 1 hour to

CONSOLIDATION

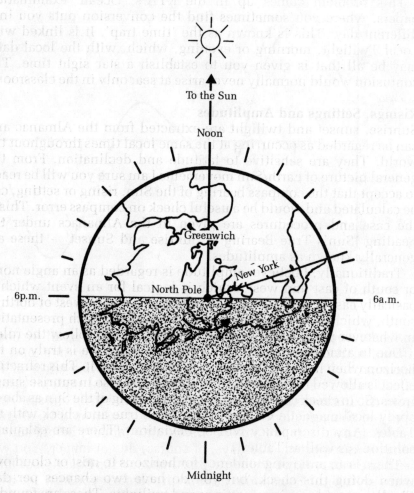

Fig 56 Time depends on longitude: when it's noon at Greenwich, it is 7am
in New York (longitude 73°50'W) and midnight at 180° longitude. As the
Earth rotates, the Sun and clock-face remain fixed and the time at Greenwich
and New York moves on; however, the difference between Greenwich time
and New York time does not change, and this difference can be used to
measure the longitude.

obtain GMT, so standard French times are 1 hour *ahead* of GMT and
equate to British Summer Time. The French, however, have
Summer Time as well! You can see that establishing GMT, which
navigational sums require, can be tricky in distant longitudes and it
is necessary to think of time as date-hours-minutes-seconds,
remembering that days start at midnight and not noon.

This problem comes up in the RYA's 'Ocean' examination papers, where you sometimes find the conversion puts you in a different day. This is known as the 'time trap'. It is linked with Local Twilight, morning or evening, which, with the local date, may be all that is given you to establish a star sight time. The confusion would normally never arise at sea; only in the classroom.

Risings, Settings and Amplitudes

Sunrise, sunset and twilight are extracted from the Almanac and can be regarded as occurring at the same local times throughout the world. They are sensitive to latitude and declination. From the general picture of Earth/Sun movements I am sure you will be ready to accept that the compass bearing of the Sun, rising or setting, can be calculated and would be a useful check on compass error. This is the case and procedures are given in the Almanacs under the heading 'Sun's True Bearing at Sunrise and Sunset' – these are generally known as amplitudes.

Traditionally, I believe, amplitude is regarded as an angle north or south of east and west, which is logical for an event which is basically east or west. It can also be given as east or west of north or south, which is more conventional for bearings. Each presentation in whatever publication is perfectly clear, so just follow the rules.

Due to atmospheric refraction, the Sun's middle is truly on the horizon when it is visually half its diameter above it. This refraction effect is allowed for in sextant corrections and also in sunrise/sunset times. So to check compass error, take a bearing of the Sun as above, apply local magnetic variation to bring to true and check with the Tables. Any discrepancy will be deviation. (There are calculator solutions as well as Tables.)

There is an annoying tendency for horizons to mist or cloud over when doing this check, but you do have two chances per day! Finally, consider risings, settings and twilights. These are found in *Reed's Almanac* 3:10 (Fig 57) and every sixth page onwards. The *Nautical Almanac* is more comprehensive but *Reed's* is perfectly adequate. Check on how to extract twilight, which we generally need for bodies other than the Sun so as to provide discernible horizon and star together. For a dawn shot, start early to identify the star and wait for the horizon to appear. Reverse this for a dusk shot. The target twilight is when the Sun is about 6° below the horizon, known as Civil Twilight. It can be calculated for your DR position by applying local longitude to the Greenwich times of the event. Part Three amplifies this.

3:10   **JANUARY, 1991**

G.M.T.   **(31 days)**   G.M.T.

⊙ **SUN** ⊙

DATE			Equation of Time		Transit	Semi-diam.	Lat. 52°N.				Lat. Corr. to Sunrise, Sunset, etc.				
Day of																
Yr.	Mth.	Week	0 h.	12 h.			Twi-light	Sun-rise	Sun-set	Twi-light	Lat.	Twi-light	Sun-rise	Sun-set	Twi-light
			m. s.	m. s.	h. m.	'	h. m.	h. m.	h. m.	h. m.	°	h. m.	h. m.	h. m.	h. m.
1	1	Tu.	+03 10	+03 24	12 03	16.3	07 28	08 08	15 59	16 39	N70	+1 57	S.B.H.	S.B.H.	−0 56
2	2	Wed.	+03 38	+03 52	12 04	16.3	07 28	08 08	16 00	16 40	68	+1 32	+2 34	−2 33	−1 32
3	3	Th.	+04 06	+04 20	12 04	16.3	07 28	08 08	16 01	16 41	66	+1 13	+1 53	−1 53	−1 13
4	4	Fri.	+04 33	+04 47	12 05	16.3	07 28	08 08	16 02	16 43	64	+0 57	+1 25	−1 25	−0 57
5	5	Sat.	+05 01	+05 14	12 05	16.3	07 27	08 07	16 03	16 44	62	+0 44	+1 04	−1 04	−0 44
6	6	Sun.	+05 28	+05 41	12 06	16.3	07 27	08 07	16 04	16 45	N60	+0 32	+0 47	−0 47	−0 33
7	7	Mon.	+05 54	+06 07	12 06	16.3	07 27	08 07	16 06	16 46	58	+0 22	+0 33	−0 32	−0 23
8	8	Tu.	+06 20	+06 33	12 07	16.3	07 26	08 06	16 07	16 47	56	+0 14	+0 21	−0 20	−0 14
9	9	Wed.	+06 46	+06 58	12 07	16.3	07 26	08 06	16 08	16 48	54	+0 07	+0 10	−0 09	−0 07
10	10	Th.	+07 11	+07 23	12 07	16.3	07 26	08 06	16 10	16 50	50	−0 06	−0 08	+0 09	+0 06
11	11	Fri.	+07 35	+07 47	12 08	16.3	07 25	08 05	16 11	16 51	N45	−0 20	−0 26	+0 27	+0 20
12	12	Sat.	+07 59	+08 11	12 08	16.3	07 25	08 04	16 13	16 52	40	−0 33	−0 41	+0 42	+0 32
13	13	Sun.	+08 22	+08 34	12 09	16.3	07 24	08 03	16 14	16 54	35	−0 43	−0 54	+0 54	+0 42
14	14	Mon.	+08 45	+08 56	12 09	16.3	07 23	08 02	16 16	16 55	30	−0 52	−0 05	+1 05	+0 52
15	15	Tu.	+09 07	+09 18	12 09	16.3	07 23	08 02	16 18	16 56	20	−1 08	−0 24	+1 24	+1 08
16	16	Wed.	+09 28	+09 39	12 10	16.3	07 22	08 01	16 19	16 58	N10	−1 24	−1 41	+1 41	+1 24
17	17	Th.	+09 49	+09 59	12 10	16.3	07 21	08 00	16 21	16 59	0	−1 39	−1 56	+1 56	+1 39
18	18	Fri.	+10 09	+10 19	12 10	16.3	07 20	07 59	16 23	17 01	S10	−1 55	−2 13	+2 11	+1 55
19	19	Sat.	+10 29	+10 38	12 11	16.3	07 19	07 58	16 24	17 02	20	−2 14	−2 30	+2 28	+2 14
20	20	Sun.	+10 47	+10 56	12 11	16.3	07 18	07 57	16 26	17 04	30	−2 36	−2 49	+2 48	+2 36
21	21	Mon.	+11 05	+11 14	12 11	16.3	07 17	07 56	16 28	17 06	S35	−2 49	−3 01	+3 00	+2 49
22	22	Tu.	+11 22	+11 30	12 12	16.3	07 16	07 54	16 29	17 07	40	−3 06	−3 15	+3 13	+3 06
23	23	Wed.	+11 38	+11 46	12 12	16.3	07 15	07 53	16 31	17 09	45	−3 26	−3 31	+3 29	+3 26
24	24	Th.	+11 54	+12 01	12 12	16.3	07 14	07 52	16 33	17 11	S50	−3 51	−3 51	+3 49	+3 52
25	25	Fri.	+12 08	+12 15	12 12	16.3	07 13	07 51	16 34	17 12					
26	26	Sat.	+12 22	+12 29	12 12	16.3	07 12	07 50	16 36	17 14					
27	27	Sun.	+12 35	+12 42	12 13	16.3	07 11	07 48	16 38	17 16			NOTES		
28	28	Mon.	+12 48	+12 54	12 13	16.3	07 09	07 47	16 39	17 17		The corrections to sunrise, sunset, etc.,			
29	29	Tu.	+12 59	+13 05	12 13	16.3	07 08	07 45	16 41	17 19		are for Jan. 15.			
30	30	Wed.	+13 10	+13 15	12 13	16.3	07 07	07 44	16 43	17 21		S.B.H. = The Sun is below the Horizon.			
31	31	Th.	+13 20	+13 24	12 13	16.3	07 05	07 42	16 45	17 22		Examples on the use of the above data			

Equation of Time is the excess of Mean Time over Apparent Time
(See explanation and examples on p. 2:15)

are given on page 2:11 onwards.

Fig 57   Reed's Almanac 3:10

Sidereal Time and Star Time

We now have to distinguish between solar time and sidereal time –
another case of 'relative motion'. While it is a convenient premise to
regard a solar day as a 360° rotation of the Earth, meridian to
meridian, outside the cosy Solar System this would be seen to be
untrue. Each day the Earth has moved along its solar orbit and
it requires a little more rotation than 360° to bring yesterday's
meridian back under it, thus concluding a solar day. Four minutes
of time does this. Fig 58 shows this as a simplified notion. A true
360° Earth rotation brings an Earth point back to the same galactic
point and defines a sidereal day of 23h 56mins. Sidereal time starts
at the first point of Aries and has its own hour angle from
Greenwich. GHA Aries is given in the Almanac alongside GHA Sun
and is used for star calculations.

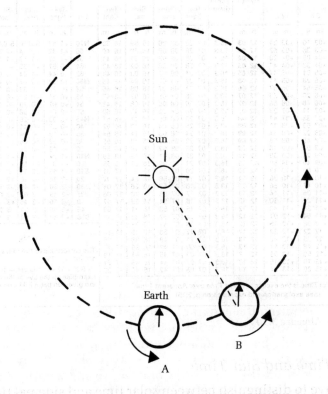

Fig 58 *When the Earth is at A, the star and the Sun are in the same direction. One sidereal day later, the Earth has moved to B; the star is still in the same direction (or it would be if the diagram was drawn to scale, with the star very, very far away) but the Sun is about one degree wrong, so a further 4 minutes will elapse before a solar day is completed.*

The stars are mercifully fixed in space and each star's hour angle, known as the sidereal hour angle, is constant from Aries – always measured westward to 360°. This four minutes we speak of means that the difference between solar time and sidereal time is exactly one day per year.

CONSOLIDATION

Lunar Time

The same mechanism is responsible for the lunar time of one month, and the tidal cycles of springs and neaps. The Moon takes a month (a 'moonth') to orbit the Earth in the same direction as the Earth's spin.

High water at a place is 50 minutes later each day, so the cycle returns to square one in 28¼ days.

More on the Sextant

Part One treated the sextant on a 'need to know' basis for Sun sights. We need to go on, to show how it works and discuss other uses.

How it Works

Fig 59 shows that although sunshine envelopes half the spinning Earth, its rays have a definite direction at any instant and each perceived ray arriving at a place is parallel to all others. Fig 59 shows a sextant shot being taken with the now well-understood objective of measuring the angle from the Earth's centre between the observer and the Sun's geographical position (the zenith distance). Isolate two of these parallel rays – one arriving at the foot of the observer, whose angle above the horizon he measures, and the other penetrating the geographical position of the Sun *en route* to the Earth's centre. Both rays meet the observer's zenith line at the same angle simply because geometry tells us parallel lines meet a common line at the same angle, and it's fairly obvious anyway.

The 90° arc from the observer's horizon to his zenith is intercepted by his sextant angle. The lower angle is his sextant angle, which, when corrected and subtracted from 90°, gives the zenith distance. This is manifestly what we are seeking – the angular distance from the observer to the geographical position of the Sun, *along the common great circle between them.*

Now, if their common great circle is a meridian in the Northern Hemisphere with the Sun due south, as shown, then we only need to look up the Sun's declination at time of sight, add it to the zenith distance and obtain latitude. If the Sun is not on the observer's meridian, the zenith distance will be the angular length of one side of the navigational spherical triangle, solved by Tables or calculator. All this is just another way of looking at the noon sight and consolidating our understanding of zenith distance.

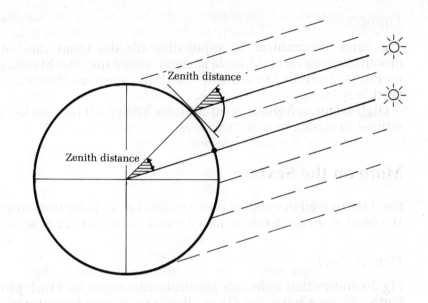

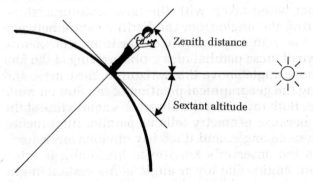

Fig 59   90° – Sextant altitude = zenith distance.
Zenith distance = length of arc from observer to GP of body.

The reader will understand, as explained in Part One, that the observer can be in north or south latitude while the Sun is north or south declination. What is said here applies to Fig 59 as shown.

Polaris
The sextant altitude of Polaris, the North Star, equals the observer's latitude. This is easy to grasp if you realize that, because of its

position, you are on a common great circle wherever you are. All roads lead to Rome! Calculating its zenith distance would be easy, and if you then subtract from 90° you would get latitude. But you subtracted the sextant altitude from 90° to get the zenith distance so it cancels it out! Can you now accept that corrected sextant altitude *is* latitude? *Reed's Almanac* 5:17 shows how to handle this as Polaris needs a slight correction. I find Polaris a bit dim to use in lower latitudes, such as the Mediterranean, where it could be useful, but it is the principle that counts.

Position Circles

We tend to think of navigational exercises as generating position lines (straight lines), but there are valuable position lines which are arcs of circles. You will remember that a celestial position line is part of a circle, but of such an immense radius it would be absurd to treat our required part of it as anything but a straight line.

The sextant can be used for terrestrial observations which provide useful circles of position. Perhaps the most obvious is measuring small vertical angles such as the height of charted objects such as lighthouses. *Reed's Almanac* 7:16 (Fig 60) shows how this technique gives distance off and the concept is readily understood and most useful in practice. We establish a radial distance off – a lighthouse, for example – and then take a bearing of it with the hand bearing-compass. Plot the back bearing and then mark the distance off and you have a fix. Remember that index error is very important here as we are dealing with small angles and short distances. As a last example of the vertical mode, you can measure the masthead to water-line angle of boats ahead or astern, and check who is gaining or falling astern.

Less easy to grasp, but extremely useful, is the generation of position circles by horizontal sextant angles. It is a refinement of fixes by back bearings from charted objects. But, whereas a hand bearing-compass can only be read to a few degrees, the sextant will read to a fraction of a degree.

There are some quirks of sextant handling which tend to be confused by explanation, but consider this. When you bring the lower limb of the Sun down to kiss the horizon, you cannot look directly at the Sun, so you estimate its angle above the horizon, set it on the sextant scale, and fish around until it appears. Then go on from there having captured it. You do not have this constraint with horizontal angles but there are other problems.

Say you have picked up two charted objects which lend them-

TABLE FOR FINDING DISTANCE OFF WITH SEXTANT
UP TO 6 MILES

Distance in Miles & Cables	HEIGHT OF OBJECT, TOP LINE METRES — LOWER LINE FEET												Distance in Miles & Cables
	12 40	15 50	18 60	21 70	24 80	27 90	30 100	33 110	37 120	40 130	43 140	46 150	
m c	° ′	° ′	° ′	° ′	° ′	° ′	° ′	° ′	° ′	° ′	° ′	° ′	m c
0 1	3 46	4 42	5 38	6 34	7 30	8 25	9 20	10 15	11 10	12 04	12 58	13 52	0 1
0 2	1 53	2 21	2 49	3 18	3 46	4 14	4 42	5 10	5 38	6 06	6 34	7 02	0 2
0 3	1 15	1 34	1 53	2 12	2 31	2 49	3 08	3 27	3 46	4 05	4 23	4 42	0 3
0 4	0 57	1 11	1 25	1 39	1 53	2 07	2 21	2 35	2 49	3 04	3 18	3 32	0 4
0 5	0 45	0 57	1 08	1 19	1 30	1 42	1 53	2 04	2 16	2 27	2 38	2 49	0 5
0 6	0 38	0 47	0 57	1 06	1 15	1 25	1 34	1 44	1 53	2 02	2 12	2 21	0 6
0 7	0 32	0 40	0 48	0 57	1 05	1 13	1 21	1 29	1 37	1 45	1 53	2 01	0 7
0 8	0 28	0 35	0 42	0 49	0 57	1 04	1 11	1 18	1 25	1 32	1 39	1 46	0 8
0 9	0 25	0 31	0 38	0 44	0 50	0 57	1 03	1 09	1 15	1 22	1 28	1 34	0 9
1 0	0 23	0 28	0 34	0 40	0 45	0 51	0 57	1 02	1 08	1 14	1 19	1 25	1 0
1 1	0 21	0 26	0 31	0 36	0 41	0 46	0 51	0 57	1 02	1 07	1 12	1 17	1 1
1 2	0 19	0 24	0 28	0 33	0 38	0 42	0 47	0 52	0 57	1 01	1 06	1 11	1 2
1 3	0 17	0 22	0 26	0 30	0 35	0 39	0 44	0 48	0 52	0 57	1 01	1 05	1 3
1 4	0 16	0 20	0 24	0 28	0 32	0 36	0 40	0 44	0 48	0 53	0 57	1 01	1 4
1 5	0 15	0 19	0 23	0 26	0 30	0 34	0 38	0 41	0 45	0 49	0 53	0 57	1 5
1 6	0 14	0 18	0 21	0 25	0 28	0 32	0 35	0 39	0 42	0 46	0 49	0 53	1 6
1 7	0 13	0 17	0 20	0 23	0 27	0 30	0 33	0 37	0 40	0 43	0 47	0 50	1 7
1 8	0 13	0 16	0 19	0 22	0 25	0 28	0 31	0 35	0 38	0 41	0 44	0 47	1 8
1 9	0 12	0 15	0 18	0 21	0 24	0 27	0 30	0 33	0 36	0 39	0 42	0 45	1 9
2 0	0 11	0 14	0 17	0 20	0 23	0 25	0 28	0 31	0 34	0 37	0 40	0 42	2 0
2 1	0 10	0 14	0 16	0 19	0 22	0 24	0 27	0 30	0 32	0 35	0 38	0 40	2 1
2 2	0 10	0 13	0 15	0 18	0 21	0 23	0 26	0 28	0 31	0 33	0 36	0 39	2 2
2 3	0 10	0 12	0 14	0 17	0 20	0 22	0 25	0 27	0 30	0 32	0 34	0 37	2 3
2 4	0 10	0 12	0 14	0 17	0 19	0 21	0 24	0 26	0 28	0 31	0 33	0 35	2 4
2 5	0 9	0 11	0 13	0 16	0 18	0 20	0 23	0 25	0 27	0 29	0 32	0 34	2 5
2 6	0 9	0 11	0 13	0 15	0 17	0 20	0 22	0 24	0 26	0 28	0 30	0 33	2 6
2 7	0 9	0 10	0 12	0 15	0 17	0 19	0 21	0 23	0 25	0 27	0 29	0 31	2 7
2 8	0 8	0 10	0 12	0 14	0 16	0 18	0 20	0 22	0 24	0 26	0 28	0 30	2 8
2 9	0 8	0 10	0 11	0 14	0 16	0 18	0 20	0 21	0 23	0 25	0 27	0 29	2 9
3 0	0 8	0 9	0 10	0 13	0 15	0 17	0 19	0 21	0 23	0 24	0 26	0 28	3 0
3 2				0 12	0 14	0 16	0 18	0 19	0 21	0 23	0 25	0 27	3 2
3 4				0 12	0 13	0 15	0 17	0 18	0 20	0 22	0 23	0 25	3 4
3 6				0 11	0 13	0 14	0 16	0 17	0 19	0 20	0 22	0 24	3 6
3 8				0 10	0 12	0 13	0 15	0 16	0 18	0 19	0 21	0 22	3 8
4 0				0 10	0 11	0 13	0 14	0 16	0 17	0 18	0 20	0 21	4 0
4 2						0 12	0 14	0 15	0 16	0 17	0 19	0 20	4 2
4 4						0 12	0 13	0 14	0 15	0 17	0 18	0 19	4 4
4 6						0 11	0 13	0 14	0 15	0 16	0 17	0 18	4 6
4 8						0 11	0 12	0 13	0 14	0 15	0 16	0 18	4 8
5 0						0 10	0 11	0 12	0 14	0 15	0 16	0 17	5 0
5 2								0 12	0 13	0 14	0 15	0 16	5 2
5 4								0 12	0 13	0 14	0 15	0 16	5 4
5 6								0 11	0 12	0 13	0 14	0 15	5 6
5 8								0 11	0 12	0 13	0 14	0 15	5 8
6 0								0 10	0 11	0 12	0 13	0 14	6 0

Fig 60 Reed's Almanac *7:16*

CONSOLIDATION

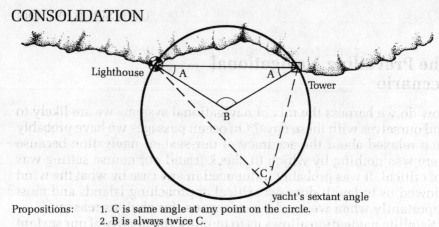

Fig 61   Circles of position (from horizontal sextant angles).

Propositions: 1. C is same angle at any point on the circle.
2. B is always twice C.
3. Included angles of any triangle = 180°.
4. Both As are equal.

Prove that A = 90° – C (A allows construction of circle)

$$2A + B = 180°$$
$$B = 2C$$
$$2A + 2C = 180°$$
Halve both sides $$A + C = 90°$$
$$A = 90° - C \quad QED$$

selves to this exercise (*see* Fig 61). You are going to measure the angle between them, free from any problems with variation or deviation. Take the sextant, check the index error, and turn it clockwise horizontally, usually right-hand down. Set to zero and pick up the right-hand object (say, a lighthouse) then gradually extend the arc to follow the reflected image to the left-hand object. It can be tricky. You can lose the image, but persevere and it is easy with practice. So you have measured angle C in Fig 61. Join the two objects with a line on the chart, subtract angle C from 90°, and lay this off as angles A as shown to produce point B where they cross. With B as centre and either A as radius, draw the position circle. You are somewhere on it.

All this works from two simple properties of chords (AA) of circles. Angle C is the same for any point on the circle. Angle B is twice angle C. (Included angles of a triangle total 180°.) So B equals 2C and both As are equal, and 2C plus 2A equals 180°. Halve this, so C plus A equals 90°, or A = 90° – C.

There are other solutions, but the above proof is rarely explained. It is fair to say that some very expert sailors prefer to plot the sextant angles on kitchen paper and line them up on the chart. Here, I am only concerned with the sextant application, leading to fluency in its use and increased affection for it.

The Prevailing Navigational Scenario

How do we harness the mix of navigational systems we are likely to find ourselves with these days? On ocean passages we have probably been relaxed about the accuracy of our sextant navigation because there was nothing by which to check it and our course setting was not critical. It was probably influenced in any case by what the wind allowed us to lay. It does get critical approaching islands and most importantly when we need a rendezvous, for obvious reasons.

Satellite navigation allows us to monitor the quality of our sextant work and to evaluate our DR between shots. This quantitative refinement of our primary navigation is one aspect. Another is the value of satellite navigation when the Sun is obscured, with its corollary of the value of a Sun sight when the electronic system is down.

The DR course and distance in a Sun-Run-Sun is strictly an estimated position (EP) because it includes leeway and current. So we are led to confidence levels which diminish after, say, six hours. The terms DR, EP and fixes are puzzles in semantics. A running fix is often less convincing than an EP based on a calibrated log and a

Fig 62   A mountain tip is a navigational bonus.

CONSOLIDATION

Fig 63   A comforting position check.

properly checked compass, driven by a good autohelm.

Offshore passages are great for sorting out DR variables against Decca, for example, but it takes effort. Properly applied you can build up data previously unobtainable. You might conclude that the last watch increased leeway by oversheeting the sails!

Log Books and Log Keeping

A log book seems to have three functions: it allows you to bring your present passage to a successful conclusion; it provides data for subsequent analysis and consideration; and, as a legal document, it should be available in the event of an inquiry.

So how does the scenario outlined in the previous section affect your log keeping? With the mixed systems outlined, you will have a plethora of plottable data and recordable events, so set up a clear working system. On a Yachtmaster Practical Assessment you lose marks if an oncoming navigator cannot pick up all he wants from log and chart without talking to the last person who used it. (The new chap says the last chap has left a muddle and is himself accused of being thick!)

Some plot Decca positions and waypoints only, with a kind of mental DR (the 'Nadger' is useful here). If you plot Course Made Good (CMG) from Decca, remember its limitations and possible confusion with other courses. The skipper has to decide on log headings which do not overwhelm the crew. If the yacht carries significant masthead instrumentation, this will influence the headings – for example, VMG instruments. On ocean passage you have to consider zone times, but keep one watch on GMT. Some skippers keep the log in GMT – very confusing in 60° west!

If you are running checks on one system against another, keep the exercises separate, and always have a separate Sight Book.

Eventually we are likely to follow aerospace practice, where primary navigation passes to electronics and space systems. However, the intellectual satisfaction and direct benefits of sextant navigation should prevail for quite a while.

So, where do these reflections lead? Log, leadline and compass navigation has gone for most of us, except the impecunious tyro who is probably back to our own starting point. We are not yet able to grab a pocket device giving an instantaneous position, and when we are, some of the magic will have gone and the stars will lose interest in us. There is a rich field in the immediate years ahead in

Fig 64   We really need an horizon – have to wait!

CONSOLIDATION

Fig 65   The author keeps his hand in.

Fig 66 Journey's end (Plymouth). Assemble all duty-free openly and tidily. Make it easy for customs men to do their job – generous treatment invariably follows.

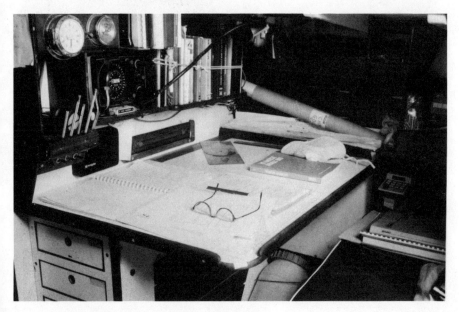

Fig 67 A traditional layout on a 56ft ocean cruiser.

which we can dabble as inclination takes us. I suppose the classic questions remain: 'Where are we now?', 'Where do we go from here?' Ninety per cent of our effort used to be devoted to the first question, and it is still the most interesting.

Summary of Part Two

This covered the theoretical principles on which certain navigational techniques are based, and several additional practices are explained with emphasis on practical application. The relevant motions of the heavenly bodies, and the various forms of time measurement are discussed.

Some chartwork aids developed by the author are illustrated and he concludes with reflections on the changing scene and the way ahead.

The occasional light-hearted touch should not obscure the cogency of the points made.

Part Three: The Moon, Planets and Stars

These bodies have been left to this stage so as not to muddy the waters of the main objective – the Sun sights. This section is a working treatise, so we are back to Flowchart B (Fig 2, *see* page 12) as there is much in common with previous coverage. We shoot the body and time it as before, then hunt for the azimuth and intercept via LHA, declination and latitude. These bodies are a rich field for the RYA 'Ocean' courses and examinations, and this coverage is designed to help students of these and similar bodies. Many who have successfully taken these courses are hesitant to tackle the Moon, planets and stars in real life. I understand that there is a limited window of twilight to shoot them and the calculations are slightly different. Don't let that put you off – there is a great range of interest and the surprisingly frequent chance of multiple shots. Sun-Moon-planet sights broaden the operating window and provide fixes instead of a position line. The fix is called an Observed Position.

You might want to extend your publications to include the *Nautical Almanac*, which is used for RYA courses. Extracts are included in the RYA Course Notes.

The same nodal points of the flowchart are, in general, valid and I shall concentrate on differences between them when they occur.

The Moon

The treatment of the Moon is influenced by the following factors:

1. We sometimes see only the lower limb or upper limb.
2. Its nearness to Earth introduces a correction for parallax.
3. It has rapid movement and declination up to 29°.
4. Calculating its time of meridian passage is slightly different.

Much of the resistance to taking Moon shots arises from lack of clarity on these points – another challenge! The RYA 'Ocean'

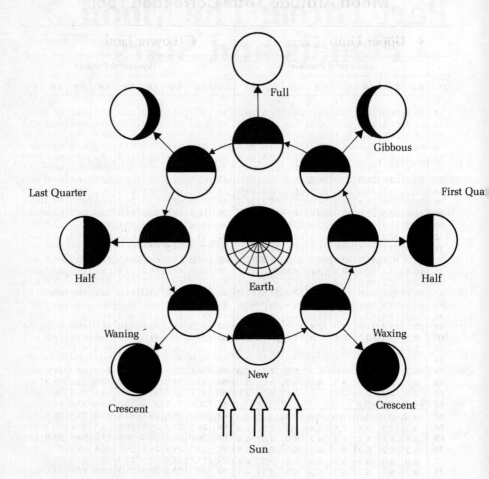

Fig 68   The phases of the Moon.

Examination often entails three stars and the Moon, which is another good reason to tackle it. First accept that the Moon uses the same publications as the Sun and is treated in much the same way along the flowpath. So, let us consider the above list.

Upper/Lower Limb – Sextant Correction

The Sun and Moon have significant observed diameters of about 0.5° and in principle upper/lower limbs of each can be taken. You have to be pretty desperate to need the Sun's upper limb but Fig 68 shows, and experience confirms, that often only one limb of the

Moon Altitude Total Correction Table

(Upper Limb Add/Subtract)								(Lower Limb Add)							
Horizontal Parallax								**Horizontal Parallax**							
Obs. Alt. 54'	55'	56'	57'	58'	59'	60'	61'	Obs. Alt. 54'	55'	56'	57'	58'	59'	60'	61'
10 23.4	24.0	24.6	25.5	26.0	26.7	27.5	28.3	10 52.7	54.0	55.3	56.5	57.7	59.0	60.2	61.5
12 23.8	24.6	25.2	26.0	26.5	27.2	28.0	28.7	12 53.2	54.5	55.7	57.0	58.4	59.5	60.7	62.0
14 24.0	24.8	25.4	26.1	26.7	27.5	28.3	29.0	14 53.5	54.7	56.0	57.3	58.5	59.8	61.0	62.3
16 24.0	24.8	25.5	26.1	26.7	27.5	28.3	28.8	16 53.5	54.6	56.0	57.3	58.5	59.8	61.0	62.2
18 23.8	24.6	25.2	26.0	26.5	27.3	28.0	28.6	18 53.4	54.6	55.7	57.0	58.4	59.5	60.6	62.0
20 23.6	24.2	25.0	25.5	26.2	27.0	27.5	28.2	20 53.0	54.4	55.5	56.8	58.0	59.0	60.4	61.5
22 23.2	23.8	24.6	25.0	25.7	26.5	27.0	27.8	22 52.5	53.7	55.0	56.3	57.5	58.8	60.0	61.0
24 22.7	23.2	24.0	24.5	25.3	25.8	26.5	27.0	24 52.0	53.3	54.5	55.5	56.7	58.0	59.4	60.5
26 22.0	22.6	23.4	24.0	24.5	25.0	25.7	26.5	26 51.5	52.5	53.7	55.0	56.3	57.5	58.0	59.8
28 21.4	22.0	22.6	23.3	23.8	24.5	25.0	25.5	28 50.7	52.0	53.0	54.4	55.5	56.5	57.8	59.0
30 20.6	21.2	21.8	22.3	23.0	23.5	24.3	24.7	30 50.0	51.0	52.3	53.5	54.5	55.7	57.0	58.0
32 19.8	20.2	21.0	21.3	22.0	22.5	23.2	23.7	32 49.3	50.4	51.3	52.5	53.7	54.8	56.0	57.0
34 19.0	19.4	20.0	20.5	21.0	21.5	22.2	22.7	34 48.3	49.5	50.5	51.5	52.7	53.7	55.0	56.0
36 18.0	18.4	19.0	19.5	20.0	20.5	21.0	21.7	36 47.3	48.5	49.5	50.5	51.7	52.7	54.0	55.0
38 16.8	17.4	17.8	18.5	19.0	19.5	20.0	20.4	38 46.4	47.4	48.5	49.5	50.5	51.5	52.7	53.8
40 15.8	16.2	16.8	17.3	17.7	18.2	18.8	19.2	40 45.3	46.3'	47.3	48.3	49.5	50.5	51.5	52.5
42 14.7	15.2	15.6	16.0	16.5	17.0	17.5	18.0	42 44.0	45.0	46.0	47.0	48.0	49.0	50.0	51.0
44 13.5	13.8	14.2	14.6	15.0	15.5	16.0	16.5	44 42.7	43.7	44.7	45.7	46.7	47.7	48.7	49.7
46 12.0	12.6	13.0	13.4	13.8	14.2	14.5	15.0	46 41.5	42.5	43.5	44.5	45.5	46.5	47.5	48.5
48 10.5	11.2	11.6	12.0	12.4	12.8	13.2	13.5	48 40.2	41.2	42.2	43.0	44.0	45.0	46.0	47.0
50 9.3	10.0	10.2	10.6	11.0	11.3	11.7	12.0	50 39.0	40.0	41.0	41.8	42.6	43.6	44.5	45.5
52 8.0	8.4	8.6	9.2	9.5	9.7	10.0	10.5	52 37.5	38.5	39.3	40.2	41.0	42.0	42.8	43.7
54 6.7	6.8	7.2	7.5	7.8	8.2	8.5	8.7	54 36.0	37.0	38.0	38.8	39.5	40.5	41.3	42.0
56 5.2	5.5	5.6	6.0	6.3	6.5	7.0	7.0	56 34.5	35.5	36.2	37.0	38.0	38.7	39.5	40.5
58 3.7	3.7	4.2	4.5	4.5	5.0	5.0	5.5	58 33.0	34.0	34.7	35.5	36.3	37.0	38.0	38.8
60 2.0	2.2	2.5	2.7	3.0	3.2	3.5	3.5	60 31.5	32.4	33.0	34.0	34.5	35.5	36.0	37.0
62 +0.5	+0.7	+0.8	+1.0	+1.2	+1.5	+1.5	+1.7	62 30.0	30.5	31.5	32.0	33.0	33.5	34.5	35.0
64 −1.2	−1.0	−1.0	−0.8	−0.6	−0.5	−0.3	−0.1	64 28.3	29.0	29.6	30.5	31.0	31.8	32.5	33.3
66 3.0	2.8	2.6	2.5	2.4	2.3	2.0	2.0	66 26.5	27.3	28.0	28.5	29.3	30.0	30.7	31.5
68 4.5	4.5	4.4	4.3	4.2	4.0	4.0	4.0	68 25.0	25.5	26.3	26.8	27.5	28.0	28.8	29.5
70 6.3	6.2	6.2	6.1	6.0	6.0	5.8	5.8	70 23.3	23.8	24.5	25.0	25.5	26.2	27.0	27.5
72 8.0	8.0	8.0	8.0	8.0	8.0	7.8	7.8	72 21.5	22.0	22.5	23.3	23.8	24.5	25.0	25.5
74 9.7	9.7	9.7	9.7	9.7	9.7	9.7	9.7	74 19.7	20.3	20.7	21.2	22.0	22.5	23.0	23.5
76 11.5	11.5	11.5	11.5	11.6	11.7	11.7	11.7	76 18.0	18.5	19.0	19.5	20.0	20.5	21.0	21.5
78 13.5	13.5	13.5	13.6	13.6	13.7	13.7	13.7	78 16.0	16.5	17.0	17.5	18.0	18.5	19.0	19.5
80 15.4	15.4	15.4	15.5	15.6	15.7	15.7	16.0	80 14.2	14.7	15.3	15.5	16.0	16.5	17.0	17.5
82 17.0	17.0	17.2	17.3	17.5	17.7	17.8	18.0	82 12.5	13.0	13.3	13.5	14.0	14.5	15.0	15.5
84 18.8	19.0	19.2	19.3	19.5	19.7	19.9	20.0	84 10.5	11.0	11.5	11.7	12.0	12.5	13.0	13.4
86 20.8	21.0	21.0	21.2	21.5	21.7	22.0	22.0	86 8.8	9.0	9.5	9.8	10.0	10.5	11.0	11.3
88 22.6	22.8	23.0	23.2	23.4	23.7	24.0	24.2	88 7.0	7.2	7.5	8.0	8.3	8.5	8.7	9.0
90								90							

HEIGHT OF EYE CORRECTION — ADD

Height of Eye in Metres	0	1.5	3	4.6	6	7.6	9	10.7	12	14	15	17	18	20	21	23	24	26	27	29	30
in feet	0	5	10	15	20	25	30	35	40	45	50	55	60	65	70	75	80	85	90	95	100
Correction +	9.8	7.6	6.7	6.0	5.5	5.0	4.5	4.0	3.5	3.2	3.0	2.5	2.3	2.0	1.7	1.3	1.0	0.8	0.5	0.2	0.0

Fig 69 Reed's Almanac 4:14.

Moon is available. So you enter the Tables with the correct one and in effect the semi-diameter correction is reversed, because it is the centre of the body we are after. Separate columns in *Reed's Almanac* deal with this (4:14 – Fig 69) and it is easy to follow. The *Nautical Almanac* covers this under 'Altitude Correction Tables – Moon'. I find *Reed's* easier. In both publications this correction is linked with horizontal parallax so we need to understand this.

Horizontal Parallax – Sextant Corrections

Fig 71 needs a brief look if you are to understand the problem and distinguish horizontal parallax from parallax in altitude. At Moon 1, its altitude is zero and parallax effect is greatest. This is termed horizontal parallax (HP). At Moon 2, parallax is reducing and this is parallax in altitude. If the Moon was overhead, then parallax would be zero (altitude 90°).

$$\text{Parallax in Altitude} = \text{Horizontal Parallax Cos Alt.}$$

If you feel you roughly understand this, don't worry about it. Simply use the Tables as directed and fetch up with true altitude.

Fig 70   A superb 'Navigatorium' on 'AYLA', a Nicholson 38 ketch.

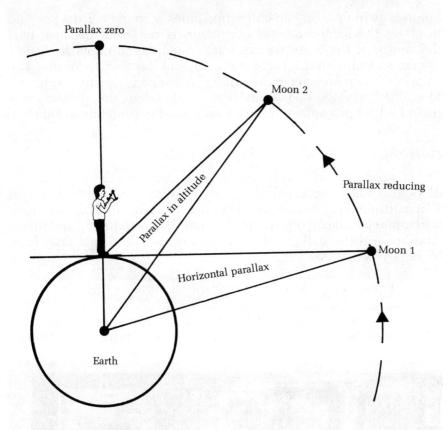

Fig 71   *The parallax effect.*

Coping with the Moon's Rapid Motion

As you would expect, this simply deals with derivation of GHA and declination, which are given at more frequent intervals to give required accuracy. *Reed's Almanac* gives the Moon's declination and GHA in 3:15, 3:21 and so on. Horizontal parallax is given in 3:10 and so on. The *Nautical Almanac* also gives clear instructions but the RYA exercises are based on examples from a past year.

Calculating Moon Time of Meridian Passage

The meridian passage of any body will give latitude, but so far we have only considered the Sun. The Moon's meridian passage

Fig 72   From left: autohelm, and the Stowe navigator, which uses masthead and underwater instrumentation for comprehensive read-outs.

Fig 73   Engine hours recorder, VHF performance monitor, radar and control panel, tailored stowage for Reed's Almanac.

Fig 74   Echo-sounder, Decca, VHF, radio/cassette player, wander light, white light, red light (car rear light).

Fig 75   Alongside the tide manual is a tailored space for the Prosser Tide Calculator.

107

Fig 76   Chris monitoring a radar extraction from a mist-enshrouded anchorage somewhere in the Aulne river, Rade de Brest.

requires you to calculate the daily difference so you can interpolate for longitude. Take your times in day-hour-minute. Say the difference is 42 minutes in your DR latitude, and your DR longitude is 149°47′ West. The longitude correction is:

$$\frac{42 \times 149°47′}{360} = 17 \text{ minutes}$$

So add that to the previous meridian passage time in day-hour-minute to get local mean time meridian passage at your DR.

I have never needed this and would just as soon have a shot at Polaris. However, it is in the RYA syllabus and becomes a mini-learning module. Both *Reed's* and the *Nautical Almanac* take you through this quite smoothly. In summary, take account of the above differences and then operate through the flowchart as for the Sun.

The Planets

Fig 77 shows the Solar System with the nine known planets. The four navigational planets are marked: Venus, Jupiter, Mars and Saturn (the *Nautical Almanac* includes Mercury). Many textbooks merely say 'extract GHA and declination from the Almanac and proceed as for the Sun', but let's go a little further.

Looking at Fig 77 gives us two mental pictures. One is our previously encouraged concept of regarding all heavenly bodies as fixed on the inner surface of a vast celestial sphere encompassing the Earth. The second is to appreciate, without sacrificing the practical value of the first, that the bodies are at enormously different distances from us. In millions of kilometres distance from the Sun, Mercury is 58, Venus 108, Earth 150, Mars 228, Jupiter 778, Saturn 1,427 and Pluto 5,900. Look also at the relative sizes of the four we use. In kilometres of diameter, Venus is 12,400, the Earth is a little larger, Mars is 6,870, Saturn is 120,000 and Jupiter is 143,000. There is no parallax or semi-diameter correction required for any.

How to Recognize the Planets

Because they wander about we can easily lose track of the planets between sailing trips. You hear people say 'Well, its either Jupiter or Venus', so it is worthwhile learning their positions so that you

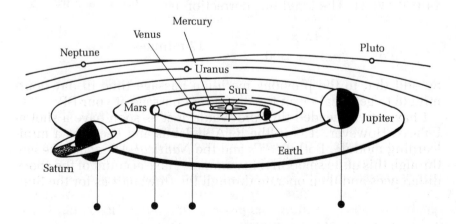

Fig 77   The Solar System – the navigational planets are indicated.

are in no doubt for the duration of the trip. I seem to manage well with Jupiter and Venus as they are so often brilliantly obvious and unencumbered by the stars when the Sun is also offering itself. Venus seems a scintillating blue, Jupiter big and steady, and Mars reddish and fainter. Planets operate about 8° either side of the ecliptic, in the zodiacal belt.

To be more scientific about recognition we use the Almanac. *Reed's Almanac* is really excellent (*see* 'How to Recognise the Planets' 2:32, and the full ephemerides on each monthly page 3:14, 3:20 and so on. Most valuable are the notes under the latter pages.) The guides include the time of meridian passage and you will gradually get a feel for helpful points, such as Venus meridian passage which is between 9a.m. and 3p.m. Regrettably, the *Nautical Almanac* treatment is difficult to absorb. The planet diagram (Fig 77) is forbidding, but no doubt the authors are proud of it. If you consider what has to go into planet data, the Almanacs are miraculous and we should be ashamed if we crib at the cost.

Planet Sight Reduction

Just a few points on sight reduction. The Almanac constructors make judgements on orbit time and so on 'as argument', and then add trimming adjustments as 'increments and corrections' – for example, *v* and *d* corrections for GHA and declination. There is no consistency in presentation and you need to note that the *v* correction for Venus in the *Nautical Almanac* is negative. The declination values are given without sign and you must check whether it is increasing or decreasing, then apply accordingly. Stick to one Almanac and it becomes simple.

Theory and Practice

For the RYA 'Ocean' papers you must cover planet meridian passage, sight reduction and sextant corrections. These just represent a few evenings' work. In practice, I suggest checking which are evening and which morning planets, and have a go at Venus and Jupiter. All the crew will get involved and it will enrich the trip. Out of interest, on 17 June 1991 there was what some regarded as an unholy conjunction of the Moon, Jupiter, Venus and Mars. Predictably, there were warnings of 'dire combustion and terrible events'. Nothing happened, and domestic hiccups earnestly reported by my family were coincidental.

The Stars

Sights taken within a few minutes can be regarded as instantaneous and, if the position lines cross at a reasonable angle, will give a fix. In coastal work we aim for three position lines, giving a cocked hat, and the third line often shows that two can be way out in the implied fix. In astro-navigation we used to aim for three, but the current RYA thinking is that four sights forming two pairs at right angles is better. Remember that a position line towards the body or its reciprocal is valid. On an ocean passage a position within 20 miles could be good enough for course shaping, but if arranging a rendezvous for assistance or to transfer a casualty, you must do a lot better. Meeting in a featureless place is the ultimate test of navigation.

Volume 1 of A.P. 3270 will offer you seven stars with three recommended for a good fix, and the RYA suggest you use four. Either way you get a fix with a high confidence, so this capability is well worth understanding and mastering.

What Stars Should We Learn?

This should be easier than it appears to be. Stars are fixed relative to each other and they wheel around the polar axis, arriving four minutes earlier each night. There are 57 navigational stars, but as a kind of snob I only deal with the bright ones. This is what I suggest we use:

Star	Constellation
Altair	Aqulia
Arcturus	Bootes
Betelgeuse	Orion
Capella	Auriga
Deneb	Cygnus
Procyon	Canis Minor
Regulus	Leo
Rigel	Orion
Sirius	Canis Major
Spica	Virgo
Vega	Lyra

Those who dissent from this list need no help from me!

Deneb, Vega and Altair form the Summer Triangle. Orion is the winter constellation. The brightest star, Sirius, is bottom left of

Orion in the UK, but top right of it in Australia. Be prepared for different aspects in different latitudes. Apart from direct recognition, stars can be identified by setting up their (roughly) calculated altitude and azimuth, when the star will appear close to the horizon when viewed in the sextant.

The steps in Flowchart A (Fig 1) remain valid in general, but there is a short cut in the offing. Taking the actual sight involves reading the scale in poor light. Sextants sometimes have a mini-light built in, but there is no real problem without it. Get the time, and carefully take the sextant to the chart table or other handy light. You probably need the telescope to brighten the image, although it cannot enlarge what is really a point source of light. You can have several minutes between shots of different bodies without compromising the principle of the 'fix'.

Previous sight reduction has conditioned us to target the GHA of a body from which we get local hour angle (LHA) and this we can do, although we shall come to a better way. Fig 78 shows that we have to 'think sidereal', and all angles are measured 360° westward. We extract GHA Aries from the Almanac, noting the nice little touch that the sign is the horns of a ram's head. Add to this figure the sidereal hour angle (SHA) of the subject star, which you also extract from the Almanac. This sum gives Greenwich hour angle star:

$$\text{GHA } \Upsilon \text{ SHA } \bigstar = \text{GHA } \bigstar$$

Having achieved GHA star, we can convert to LHA star by applying longitude (adjusting to an even number of degrees) and then process through A.P. 3270 Volume 2 or 3, according to the latitude band. This is a solid but pedestrian approach with a few extra steps and limited to bodies up to 30° declination.

Now the short cut – given that the sidereal hour angles of stars, that is their regular distance from Aries, are constant, then LHA Aries is unique for any star at a given time. So we can conceive of a set of Tables which accepts LHA Aries and outputs a number of stars, by names, which would be available to that latitude at that time. It can go further and indicate the brighter stars plus those whose crossing makes a good fix. This is exactly what Volume 1 of A.P. 3270 does.

This brilliant concept has revolutionized star sight reduction. The specification is credited to the Royal Air Force, the Royal Canadian Air Force and the United States Air Force.

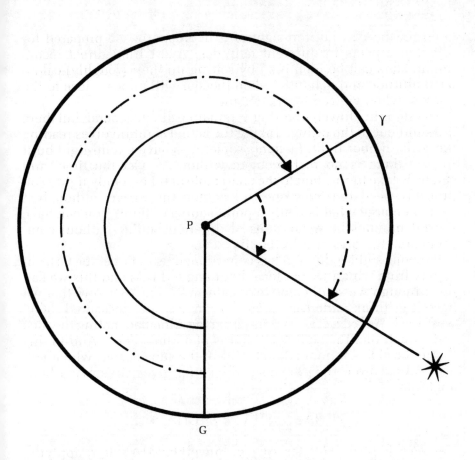

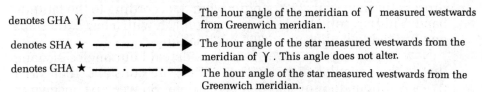

denotes GHA Υ ⟶		The hour angle of the meridian of Υ measured westwards from Greenwich meridian.
denotes SHA ★ ⟶		The hour angle of the star measured westwards from the meridian of Υ. This angle does not alter.
denotes GHA ★ ⟶		The hour angle of the star measured westwards from the Greenwich meridian.

The last angle *always* equals the sum of the other two hour angles.   GHA Υ + SHA ★ = GHA ★

Fig 78   Sidereal and related angles.

How to Use Volume 1 of A.P. 3270

The extract (Fig 79) shows a page from latitude 50°N. Above LHA Aries 15° are shown seven stars, in principle all available. Those in capitals (CAPELLA, ALDEBARAN and DENEB) are the bright ones.

Fig 79 A.P. 3270 latitude 50°N. (LAT 50°N)

LHA/γ° 0–44

LHA γ°	·CAPELLA Hc Zn	ALDEBARAN Hc Zn	Hamal Hc Zn	·Alpheratz Hc Zn	ALTAIR Hc Zn	·VEGA Hc Zn	Kochab Hc Zn
0	39 40 062	26 13 095	53 49 126	68 55 176	24 10 254	33 56 292	37 32 347
1	40 14 063	26 51 096	54 20 128	68 57 181	23 33 255	33 20 292	37 26 347
2	40 48 063	27 30 097	54 50 130	68 57 183	22 56 256	32 45 293	37 14 347
3	41 23 064	28 08 098	55 20 130	68 56 183	22 18 257	32 09 294	37 06 347
4	41 58 064	28 46 099	55 50 131	68 53 185	21 41 257	31 34 294	36 57 348
5	42 32 065	29 24 100	56 18 133	68 49 188	21 03 258	30 59 295	36 49 348
6	43 07 065	30 02 100	56 46 134	68 43 190	20 25 259	30 24 295	36 41 348
7	43 43 066	30 40 101	57 14 135	68 35 193	19 47 260	29 49 296	36 34 349
8	44 18 066	31 18 102	57 40 137	68 26 195	19 09 260	29 15 297	36 26 349
9	44 53 067	31 55 103	58 06 138	68 15 197	18 31 261	28 40 297	36 19 349
10	45 29 067	32 33 104	58 32 140	68 03 200	17 53 262	28 06 298	36 12 350
11	46 05 068	33 10 105	58 56 142	67 49 202	17 15 263	27 32 298	36 05 350
12	46 40 068	33 48 105	59 20 143	67 34 204	16 36 264	26 58 299	35 58 350
13	47 16 069	34 25 106	59 43 145	67 18 206	15 58 265	26 25 300	35 51 351
14	47 52 070	35 02 107	60 04 147	67 00 208	15 20 265	25 51 300	35 45 351

LHA γ°	·CAPELLA Hc Zn	ALDEBARAN Hc Zn	Hamal Hc Zn	·Diphda Hc Zn	Alpheratz Hc Zn	·DENEB Hc Zn	Kochab Hc Zn
15	48 29 070	35 38 108	60 25 148	21 46 185	66 41 210	47 23 290	35 39 351
16	49 05 071	36 15 109	60 44 150	21 42 186	66 21 212	46 47 290	35 33 351
17	49 41 071	36 51 110	61 03 152	21 38 187	66 00 214	46 11 291	35 28 352
18	50 18 072	37 27 111	61 21 154	21 34 188	65 37 216	45 35 291	35 23 352
19	50 54 072	38 03 112	61 38 155	21 28 189	65 14 218	44 59 292	35 17 352
20	51 31 073	38 39 113	61 53 157	21 22 190	64 50 220	44 23 292	35 12 353
21	52 08 073	39 14 114	62 07 159	21 15 191	64 27 222	43 47 293	35 07 353
22	52 45 074	39 50 115	62 21 161	21 08 192	63 58 224	43 12 293	35 02 353
23	53 22 074	40 24 116	62 32 163	21 00 193	63 31 225	42 37 294	34 58 354
24	53 59 075	40 59 117	62 43 165	20 51 194	63 04 227	42 01 294	34 54 354
25	54 37 075	41 33 118	62 52 167	20 42 195	62 35 229	41 26 295	34 50 354
26	55 14 076	42 07 119	63 00 169	20 32 196	62 06 230	40 51 295	34 46 355
27	55 51 076	42 41 120	63 07 171	20 21 197	61 36 232	40 17 296	34 43 355
28	56 29 077	43 14 121	63 13 173	20 09 198	61 05 233	39 42 296	34 39 355
29	57 06 077	43 47 122	63 18 175	19 57 199	60 34 235	39 08 297	34 36 356

LHA γ°	CAPELLA Hc Zn	·BETELGEUSE Hc Zn	RIGEL Hc Zn	Hamal Hc Zn	·Alpheratz Hc Zn	DENEB Hc Zn	·Kochab Hc Zn
30	57 44 078	25 36 115	18 15 129	63 19 177	60 03 236	38 33 297	34 33 356
31	58 22 079	26 12 116	18 45 130	63 21 179	59 30 237	37 59 298	34 31 356
32	59 00 079	26 48 117	19 15 131	63 21 181	59 00 239	37 25 299	34 28 357
33	59 38 080	27 24 118	19 44 132	63 19 183	58 24 240	36 51 299	34 26 357
34	60 16 080	27 59 119	20 12 133	63 16 185	57 51 241	36 18 300	34 24 357
35	60 54 081	28 34 115	20 41 133	63 12 187	57 17 243	35 44 300	34 22 357
36	61 32 081	29 09 116	21 08 134	63 06 189	56 42 244	35 11 301	34 20 358
37	62 10 082	29 44 117	21 36 135	63 00 191	56 08 245	34 38 301	34 19 358
38	62 48 083	30 18 118	22 03 136	62 51 193	55 33 246	34 05 302	34 18 358
39	63 26 083	30 52 119	22 29 137	62 42 195	54 57 247	33 32 302	34 17 359
40	64 05 084	31 26 120	22 55 138	62 31 197	54 21 248	33 00 303	34 16 359
41	64 43 084	31 59 121	23 20 139	62 19 199	53 46 249	32 28 303	34 16 359
42	65 22 085	32 33 122	23 45 140	62 06 201	53 09 250	31 55 304	34 16 000
43	66 00 086	33 05 122	24 10 141	61 52 203	52 33 251	31 24 304	34 15 000
44	66 38 086	33 37 123	24 34 142	61 36 205	51 56 253	30 52 305	34 16 000

LHA/γ° 90–134

LHA γ°	·Dubhe Hc Zn	REGULUS Hc Zn	PROCYON Hc Zn	·SIRIUS Hc Zn	RIGEL Hc Zn	ALDEBARAN Hc Zn	·Mirfak Hc Zn
90	48 42 044	27 15 104	40 46 147	22 37 169	30 53 193	52 17 215	64 56 285
91	49 09 044	27 52 105	41 07 148	22 44 170	30 44 195	51 55 216	64 19 285
92	49 35 044	28 29 106	41 27 149	22 51 171	30 34 196	51 32 218	63 41 286
93	50 02 044	29 06 107	41 46 151	22 57 172	30 24 197	51 08 219	63 04 286
94	50 29 045	29 43 108	42 05 152	23 02 173	30 11 198	50 43 220	62 27 286
95	50 57 045	30 20 109	42 22 153	23 06 174	29 59 199	50 18 222	61 50 287
96	51 24 045	30 56 110	42 39 155	23 11 175	29 46 200	49 51 223	61 13 287
97	51 51 045	31 32 111	42 56 156	23 14 177	29 32 201	49 25 224	60 37 288
98	52 19 045	32 08 111	43 11 157	23 16 178	29 18 202	48 57 226	60 00 288
99	52 46 045	32 44 112	43 26 159	23 18 178	29 03 204	48 30 227	59 23 289
100	53 14 046	33 20 113	43 39 160	23 19 179	28 47 205	48 01 228	58 47 289
101	53 41 046	33 56 114	43 52 161	23 19 180	28 31 206	47 32 230	58 10 289
102	54 09 046	34 30 115	44 04 163	23 18 181	28 14 207	47 02 231	57 34 290
103	54 37 046	35 05 116	44 15 164	23 16 182	27 56 208	46 32 232	56 58 290
104	55 05 046	35 40 117	44 25 165	23 16 183	27 38 209	46 02 233	56 22 291

LHA γ°	·Dubhe Hc Zn	Denebola Hc Zn	REGULUS Hc Zn	·SIRIUS Hc Zn	RIGEL Hc Zn	ALDEBARAN Hc Zn	·Mirfak Hc Zn
105	55 33 047	22 47 094	36 14 118	23 14 184	27 19 210	45 31 234	55 46 291
106	56 01 047	23 24 095	36 48 119	23 10 185	26 59 211	45 00 235	55 10 292
107	56 29 047	24 04 096	37 21 120	23 07 186	26 39 212	44 27 237	54 34 292
108	56 57 047	24 42 097	37 54 122	23 02 187	26 18 213	43 55 238	53 58 292
109	57 25 047	25 20 097	38 27 122	22 57 188	25 57 214	43 23 239	53 23 293
110	57 53 047	25 59 098	39 00 123	22 51 189	25 35 215	42 49 240	52 47 293
111	58 21 047	26 37 099	39 32 124	22 44 190	25 12 216	42 15 241	52 12 294
112	58 50 047	27 15 100	40 04 125	22 37 191	24 49 217	41 41 242	51 37 294
113	59 18 047	27 53 101	40 35 126	22 29 192	24 26 218	41 07 243	51 01 295
114	59 46 047	28 31 101	41 06 127	22 20 193	24 02 219	40 33 244	50 26 295
115	60 14 047	29 08 102	41 36 128	22 11 194	23 37 220	39 58 245	49 51 295
116	60 43 047	29 46 103	42 06 130	22 01 195	23 12 221	39 23 246	49 17 296
117	61 11 047	30 24 104	42 36 131	21 50 196	22 46 222	38 48 247	48 42 296
118	61 39 047	31 01 105	43 05 132	21 39 197	22 20 223	38 12 248	48 08 297
119	62 08 047	31 38 106	43 33 133	21 27 199	21 54 224	37 36 249	47 33 297

LHA γ°	Kochab Hc Zn	Denebola Hc Zn	·REGULUS Hc Zn	SIRIUS Hc Zn	RIGEL Hc Zn	·ALDEBARAN Hc Zn	CAPELLA Hc Zn
120	44 21 022	32 15 107	44 01 134	21 15 200	21 27 225	37 00 250	62 26 278
121	44 35 022	32 52 107	44 28 136	21 01 201	20 59 226	36 24 251	61 48 278
122	44 50 022	33 30 109	44 55 137	20 48 202	20 30 227	35 47 252	61 10 279
123	45 04 022	34 05 109	45 21 138	20 33 203	20 03 228	35 11 253	60 32 279
124	45 19 022	34 42 110	45 47 139	20 18 204	19 34 229	34 34 253	59 54 280
125	45 34 023	35 18 111	46 11 141	20 02 204	19 05 230	33 57 254	59 16 281
126	45 48 023	35 53 112	46 36 142	19 46 205	18 35 231	33 20 255	58 38 281
127	46 03 023	36 29 113	46 59 143	19 29 206	18 05 231	32 42 256	58 00 282
128	46 18 023	37 05 114	47 22 144	19 12 207	17 35 232	32 05 257	57 22 282
129	46 34 023	37 40 115	47 44 146	18 54 208	17 04 233	31 27 258	56 45 283
130	46 49 023	38 14 116	48 05 147	18 35 209	16 33 234	30 49 259	56 07 283
131	47 04 023	38 48 117	48 25 149	18 16 210	16 02 235	30 11 259	55 30 284
132	47 20 024	39 23 118	48 46 150	17 56 211	15 30 236	29 33 260	54 52 284
133	47 35 024	39 57 119	49 05 151	17 36 212	14 58 237	28 55 261	54 15 285
134	47 51 024	40 31 120	49 23 153	17 15 213	14 26 238	28 17 262	53 38 286

	•Dubhe	POLLUX	BETELGEUSE	•RIGEL	Hamal	•Alpheratz	DENEB
45	31 27 028	33 05 084	34 09 124	24 57 143	61 19 207	51 19 254	30 20 306
46	31 45 029	33 43 085	34 41 126	25 20 144	61 01 208	50 42 255	29 49 306
47	32 04 029	34 22 086	35 12 127	25 42 145	60 42 210	50 05 255	29 18 307
48	32 23 030	35 00 087	35 43 128	26 04 146	60 22 212	49 28 256	28 47 307
49	32 42 030	35 39 087	36 13 129	26 25 147	60 01 214	48 50 257	28 17 308
50	33 02 030	36 17 088	36 43 130	26 46 148	59 40 215	48 12 258	27 46 308
51	33 21 031	36 56 089	37 13 131	27 06 149	59 17 217	47 34 259	27 16 309
52	33 41 031	37 34 090	37 42 132	27 25 150	58 53 219	46 56 260	26 46 309
53	34 01 032	38 13 090	38 10 133	27 44 151	58 29 220	46 18 261	26 17 310
54	34 22 032	38 51 091	38 38 134	28 02 152	58 03 222	45 40 262	25 47 311
55	34 42 032	39 30 092	39 05 135	28 20 154	57 37 223	45 02 263	25 18 311
56	35 03 033	40 08 093	39 32 136	28 36 155	57 10 225	44 24 264	24 49 312
57	35 24 033	40 47 093	39 59 138	28 53 156	56 43 226	43 45 264	24 20 312
58	35 45 034	41 25 094	40 24 139	29 08 157	56 15 228	43 07 265	23 52 313
59	36 07 034	42 04 095	40 50 140	29 23 158	55 46 229	42 29 266	23 24 313
	•Dubhe	POLLUX	SIRIUS	•RIGEL	Hamal	•Alpheratz	DENEB
60	36 28 034	42 42 096	14 10 140	29 37 159	55 17 230	41 50 267	22 56 314
61	36 50 035	43 21 097	14 35 140	29 51 160	54 47 232	41 12 268	22 28 315
62	37 12 035	43 59 098	14 59 141	30 03 161	54 16 233	40 33 268	22 01 315
63	37 35 035	44 37 098	15 23 142	30 15 162	53 45 234	39 54 269	21 34 316
64	37 57 036	45 15 099	15 46 143	30 27 163	53 13 236	39 16 270	21 07 316
65	38 20 036	45 53 100	16 09 144	30 37 165	52 41 237	38 37 271	20 40 317
66	38 43 037	46 31 101	16 31 145	30 47 166	52 09 238	37 59 271	20 14 317
67	39 06 037	47 09 102	16 53 146	30 56 167	51 36 239	37 20 272	19 48 318
68	39 29 037	47 47 103	17 15 147	31 05 168	51 02 240	36 42 273	19 23 319
69	39 52 038	48 24 104	17 35 148	31 12 169	50 29 242	36 03 274	18 57 319
70	40 16 038	49 01 105	17 56 149	31 19 170	49 55 243	35 25 274	18 32 320
71	40 40 038	49 39 106	18 15 150	31 25 171	49 20 244	34 46 275	18 08 320
72	41 04 039	50 16 107	18 35 151	31 31 173	48 45 245	34 08 276	17 43 321
73	41 28 039	50 52 108	18 53 152	31 35 174	48 10 246	33 30 277	17 19 322
74	41 52 039	51 29 109	19 11 153	31 39 175	47 35 247	32 51 277	16 55 322
	•Dubhe	REGULUS	PROCYON	•SIRIUS	RIGEL	•Hamal	DENEB
75	42 17 040	17 43 092	34 22 130	19 29 154	31 42 176	46 59 248	16 32 323
76	42 41 040	18 22 093	34 51 131	19 46 155	31 44 177	46 23 249	16 09 324
77	43 06 040	19 00 094	35 20 132	20 02 155	31 46 178	45 47 250	15 46 324
78	43 31 040	19 39 095	35 49 133	20 18 156	31 46 180	45 11 251	15 24 325
79	43 56 041	20 17 095	36 17 134	20 33 157	31 46 181	44 34 252	15 02 325
80	44 22 041	20 56 096	36 44 135	20 47 158	31 45 182	43 58 253	14 40 326
81	44 47 041	21 34 097	37 11 136	21 01 159	31 43 183	43 21 254	14 18 327
82	45 13 042	22 12 098	37 37 138	21 14 160	31 41 184	42 43 255	13 57 327
83	45 38 042	22 50 099	38 03 139	21 27 161	31 38 185	42 06 256	13 37 328
84	46 04 042	23 28 099	38 28 140	21 39 162	31 34 187	41 29 257	13 16 329
85	46 30 042	24 06 100	38 53 141	21 50 163	31 29 188	40 51 258	12 56 329
86	46 56 043	24 44 101	39 17 142	22 01 164	31 23 189	40 13 258	12 37 330
87	47 22 043	25 22 102	39 40 143	22 11 165	31 17 190	39 36 259	12 18 330
88	47 49 043	26 00 103	40 03 145	22 20 167	31 10 191	38 58 260	11 59 331
89	48 15 043	26 37 103	40 25 146	22 29 168	31 02 192	38 20 261	11 40 332

	•Kochab	ARCTURUS	Denebola	•REGULUS	SIRIUS	BETELGEUSE	•CAPELLA
135	48 06 024	21 54 086	41 04 121	49 40 154	16 54 214	32 29 239	53 01 286
136	48 22 024	22 32 086	41 37 122	49 56 156	16 32 215	31 56 240	52 24 287
137	48 38 024	23 11 087	42 09 123	50 12 157	16 10 216	31 23 241	51 47 287
138	48 53 024	23 49 088	42 42 124	50 26 159	15 47 217	30 49 241	51 10 288
139	49 09 024	24 28 089	43 13 125	50 40 160	15 23 218	30 15 242	50 33 288
140	49 25 024	25 06 089	43 45 126	50 53 162	15 00 219	29 41 243	49 57 289
141	49 41 025	25 45 090	44 15 128	51 04 163	14 35 220	29 06 244	49 20 289
142	49 57 025	26 24 091	44 46 129	51 15 165	14 11 220	28 31 245	48 44 290
143	50 13 025	27 02 092	45 16 130	51 25 166	13 45 221	27 56 246	48 07 290
144	50 29 025	27 41 093	45 45 131	51 33 168	13 20 222	27 21 247	47 31 291
145	50 46 025	28 19 093	46 14 132	51 41 169	12 54 223	26 45 248	46 55 291
146	51 02 025	28 58 094	46 42 134	51 48 171	12 27 224	26 09 249	46 20 292
147	51 18 025	29 36 095	47 10 135	51 53 172	12 00 225	25 33 250	45 44 292
148	51 34 025	30 15 096	47 37 136	51 58 174	11 33 226	24 57 251	45 08 293
149	51 50 025	30 53 097	48 03 137	52 01 176	11 05 226	24 20 251	44 33 293
	•Kochab	ARCTURUS	•SPICA	REGULUS	PROCYON	•BETELGEUSE	CAPELLA
150	52 07 025	31 31 097	14 31 128	52 04 177	36 17 226	23 44 252	43 57 294
151	52 23 025	32 09 098	15 01 129	52 05 179	35 49 227	23 07 253	43 22 294
152	52 39 025	32 47 099	15 31 130	52 05 180	35 20 228	22 30 254	42 47 295
153	52 55 025	33 26 100	16 01 131	52 05 182	34 51 229	21 53 255	42 12 295
154	53 12 025	34 04 101	16 30 132	52 03 184	34 22 230	21 16 256	41 37 296
155	53 28 025	34 41 101	16 58 132	52 00 185	33 52 231	20 38 256	41 03 296
156	53 44 025	35 19 102	17 27 133	51 56 187	33 22 232	20 01 257	40 28 297
157	54 01 025	35 57 103	17 55 134	51 51 188	32 51 233	19 23 258	39 54 297
158	54 17 025	36 34 104	18 22 135	51 45 190	32 20 234	18 45 259	39 20 298
159	54 33 025	37 12 105	18 49 136	51 38 191	31 49 235	18 07 260	38 46 299
160	54 49 025	37 49 106	19 15 137	51 29 193	31 17 236	17 29 260	38 12 299
161	55 05 025	38 26 107	19 41 138	51 20 195	30 45 237	16 51 261	37 39 300
162	55 21 025	39 03 108	20 07 139	51 10 196	30 12 238	16 13 262	37 05 300
163	55 37 025	39 39 109	20 32 140	50 59 198	29 39 239	15 35 263	36 32 301
164	55 53 024	40 16 110	20 57 141	50 47 199	29 06 240	14 56 264	35 59 301
	•VEGA	ARCTURUS	•SPICA	REGULUS	PROCYON	•POLLUX	CAPELLA
165	16 00 048	40 52 111	21 21 142	50 33 201	28 32 241	47 05 258	35 26 302
166	16 28 048	41 28 111	21 45 143	50 19 202	27 58 242	46 27 259	34 53 302
167	16 57 049	42 04 112	22 08 144	50 04 204	27 24 243	45 49 260	34 21 303
168	17 27 050	42 39 113	22 30 145	49 49 205	26 50 244	45 11 261	33 48 303
169	17 56 050	43 14 114	22 52 146	49 32 207	26 15 245	44 33 262	33 16 304
170	18 26 051	43 49 116	23 14 147	49 14 208	25 40 246	43 55 262	32 44 304
171	18 56 052	44 24 117	23 35 148	48 56 209	25 05 246	43 17 263	32 12 305
172	19 27 052	44 58 118	23 55 149	48 36 211	24 29 247	42 38 264	31 41 305
173	19 57 053	45 32 119	24 15 150	48 16 212	23 54 248	42 00 265	31 09 306
174	20 28 054	46 06 120	24 34 151	47 55 214	23 18 249	41 21 266	30 38 306
175	20 59 054	46 39 121	24 52 152	47 34 215	22 42 250	40 43 267	30 07 307
176	21 31 055	47 12 122	25 10 153	47 11 216	22 05 251	40 04 267	29 37 308
177	22 02 055	47 45 123	25 28 154	46 48 218	21 29 252	39 26 268	29 06 308
178	22 34 056	48 17 124	25 45 155	46 24 219	20 52 252	38 47 269	28 36 309
179	23 06 057	48 48 125	26 01 156	46 00 220	20 15 253	38 09 270	28 06 309

60

Those starred (CAPELLA, Diphda and DENEB) give a good three-star fix. Above each column you find tabulated altitude (Hc) and Zn. Zn is the actual azimuth as a true bearing, so you don't have 'the mysteries of Z and Zn' to contend with. We will come back to this table later.

Correcting Sextant Altitude

Reed's Almanac treats this very simply in 4:6 (Fig 80). Apply index error and then enter the Tables with height of eye (dip) and the observed altitude. Correction is always negative because semidiameter, which puts in a large positive correction, for the Sun is absent. So using *Reed's Almanac* for stars, take GHA from pages 3:12, 3:13 and so on, and correct for intermediate times from the two-hour intervals by the correction Tables in 4:8 (Fig 81). Apply longitude correction, minus west, plus east to give LHA Aries for entry to Volume 1. Choose your stars and read off tabulated altitude and azimuth.

Star Sight Planning

Each twilight, morning and evening, is a potential star sight opportunity. A little planning is sensible and the RYA very properly insists that you demonstrate it. First, remember the time trap previously mentioned. The scenario given is that you have a ship's clock set to zone time, reading hours-minutes, and in 12-hour notation. You also have a deck watch set to GMT, reading hours-minutes-seconds, also in 12-hour notation with a correction table for error. All you are given is morning or evening twilight, and you have to ensure that your GMT for extracting GHA Aries is in the right day and the right 12-hour bracket.

Take this step-by-step:

Assume local Civil Twilight	22 day –	18h –	30min
Longitude as time (135°17′W) to be added:		09 –	01 –
	23 –	03 –	31 –

You *add* the time difference because you are working from west longitude to GMT ('longitude west – GMT best'). So in this case the deck watch is saying 03h, not 15.00h, and if the corrected time is not 31min but 29min 38s, then the full GMT is 23day-03h-29min-38s.

SUN ALTITUDE TOTAL CORRECTION TABLE

The Table on page 4:5 shows the combined effect of the usual Sun's corrections for Dip of the Horizon, Refraction, Parallax and Semi-Diameter. The corrections have been reduced to minutes and tenths, these tenths may be reduced to seconds by multiplying them by six.

Owing to the fact that the Table has been calculated for a fixed Semi-Diameter, it is necessary to apply a small monthly correction (given at the foot of the Table) if accuracy is desired.

If the Sun's Upper Limb has been observed, subtract twice the Sun's Semi-Diameter (given on the monthly pages) from the Altitude and then use this Table in the usual way.

Example: Having taken a Meridian Altitude of the Sun for Latitude at neon on July 20th, required the True Altitude. Height of eye 4.6 metres above the sea. Observed Altitude 42° 25.5′.

Observed Altitude of Sun's Lower Limb	42° +25.5′
Correction from Table. Alt. 43° and H.E. 4.6m (July)	+11.1′
True Altitude	42° 36.6′

STAR OR PLANET ALTITUDE TOTAL CORRECTION TABLE

ALWAYS SUBTRACTIVE (−)

Height of Eye above the Sea. Top line metres − lower line feet

Obs. Alt.	1.5	3	4.6	6	7.6	9	10.7	12	13.7	15	16.8	18	21.3
	5	10	15	20	25	30	35	40	45	50	55	60	70
9°	8.0	8.9	9.6	10.3	10.7	11.2	11.6	12.0	12.4	12.8	13.1	13.5	14.1
10°	7.4	8.4	9.1	9.7	10.2	10.6	11.1	11.5	11.8	12.2	12.5	12.9	13.5
11°	7.0	7.9	8.6	9.2	9.7	10.2	10.6	11.0	11.4	11.8	12.0	12.4	13.0
12°	6.6	7.5	8.2	8.8	9.3	9.8	10.2	10.6	11.0	11.4	11.6	12.0	12.6
13°	6.2	7.2	7.9	8.4	9.0	9.4	9.9	10.3	10.6	11.0	11.3	11.6	12.3
14°	5.9	6.9	7.6	8.1	8.6	9.2	9.6	10.0	10.3	10.7	11.0	11.3	12.0
15°	5.7	6.6	7.3	7.9	8.4	8.9	9.3	9.7	10.1	10.4	10.8	11.1	11.7
16°	5.5	6.4	7.1	7.7	8.2	8.7	9.1	9.5	9.9	10.2	10.5	10.9	11.5
17°	5.3	6.2	6.9	7.5	8.0	8.5	8.9	9.3	9.7	10.0	10.3	10.7	11.3
18°	5.1	6.0	6.7	7.3	7.8	8.3	8.7	9.1	9.5	9.8	10.2	10.5	11.1
19°	4.9	5.8	6.5	7.1	7.6	8.1	8.5	8.9	9.3	9.7	10.0	10.3	11.0
20°	4.8	5.7	6.4	7.0	7.5	8.0	8.4	8.8	9.2	9.6	9.9	10.2	10.8
25°	4.2	5.1	5.8	6.4	6.9	7.4	7.8	8.2	8.6	9.0	9.3	9.6	10.2
30°	3.8	4.7	5.4	6.0	6.5	7.0	7.4	7.8	8.2	8.6	8.9	9.2	9.8
35°	3.5	4.4	5.1	5.7	6.3	6.7	7.2	7.6	7.9	8.3	8.6	8.9	9.5
40°	3.3	4.2	4.9	5.5	6.0	6.5	6.9	7.3	7.7	8.1	8.4	8.7	9.3
50°	3.0	3.9	4.6	5.2	5.7	6.2	6.6	7.0	7.4	7.7	8.1	8.4	9.0
60°	2.7	3.6	4.4	4.9	5.5	5.9	6.4	6.8	7.1	7.5	7.8	8.1	8.8
70°	2.5	3.4	4.1	4.7	5.3	5.7	6.2	6.6	6.9	7.3	7.6	7.9	8.6
80°	2.3	3.3	4.0	4.6	5.1	5.5	6.0	6.4	6.7	7.1	7.4	7.8	8.4
90°	2.2	3.1	3.8	4.4	4.9	5.4	5.8	6.2	6.6	6.9	7.3	7.6	8.2

The above table contains the combined effects of Dip of the Horizon and Refraction and is therefore a total correction table for a Star or Planet. It is always subtractive.

Example: The observed altitude of a star was 32° 50′; and the height of observer's eye was 20 feet. What was the star's True Altitude?

Star's Observed Altitude	32° 50.0′
Correction from Table .... −	5.8′
Star's True Altitude	32° 44.2′

Fig 80   Reed's Almanac *4:6.*

Correction for DATE

Greenwich Date	Correction ° '
1st	+ 0 0.0
2nd	+ 0 59.1
3rd	+ 1 58.2
4th	+ 2 57.3
5th	+ 3 56.5
6th	+ 4 55.6
7th	+ 5 54.8
8th	+ 6 54.0
9th	+ 7 53.1
10th	+ 8 52.2
11th	+ 9 51.4
12th	+ 10 50.5
13th	+ 11 49.6
14th	+ 12 48.8
15th	+ 13 48.0
16th	+ 14 47.1
17th	+ 15 46.2
18th	+ 16 45.3
19th	+ 17 44.5
20th	+ 18 43.6
21st	+ 19 42.7
22nd	+ 20 41.9
23rd	+ 21 41.0
24th	+ 22 40.1
25th	+ 23 39.3
26th	+ 24 38.4
27th	+ 25 37.6
28th	+ 26 36.7
29th	+ 27 35.8
30th	+ 28 35.0
31st	+ 29 34.1

Correction for HOURS

Hours	Correction ° '
0	+ 0 0.0
1	+ 15 2.5
2	+ 30 4.9
3	+ 45 7.4
4	+ 60 9.9
5	+ 75 12.3
6	+ 90 14.8
7	+ 105 17.2
8	+ 120 19.7
9	+ 135 22.2
10	+ 150 24.6
11	+ 165 27.1
12	+ 180 29.6
13	+ 195 32.0
14	+ 210 34.5
15	+ 225 37.0
16	+ 240 39.4
17	+ 255 41.9
18	+ 270 44.4
19	+ 285 46.8
20	+ 300 49.3
21	+ 315 51.7
22	+ 330 54.2
23	+ 345 56.7
24	+ 360 59.1

Corr. for 1 HOUR+MIN.

1 hr. + mins.	Correction ° '
0	+ 15 2.5
1	+ 15 17.5
2	+ 15 32.6
3	+ 15 47.6
4	+ 16 2.7
5	+ 16 17.7
6	+ 16 32.7
7	+ 16 47.8
8	+ 17 2.8
9	+ 17 17.9
10	+ 17 32.9
11	+ 17 48.0
12	+ 18 3.0
13	+ 18 18.0
14	+ 18 33.1
15	+ 18 48.1
16	+ 19 3.2
17	+ 19 18.2
18	+ 19 33.2
19	+ 19 48.3
20	+ 20 3.3
21	+ 20 18.4
22	+ 20 33.4
23	+ 20 48.4
24	+ 21 3.5
25	+ 21 18.5
26	+ 21 33.6
27	+ 21 48.6
28	+ 22 3.6
29	+ 22 18.7
30	+ 22 33.7
31	+ 22 48.8
32	+ 23 3.8
33	+ 23 18.9
34	+ 23 33.9
35	+ 23 48.9
36	+ 24 4.0
37	+ 24 19.0
38	+ 24 34.1
39	+ 24 49.1
40	+ 25 4.1
41	+ 25 19.2
42	+ 25 34.2
43	+ 25 49.3
44	+ 26 4.3
45	+ 26 19.3
46	+ 26 34.4
47	+ 26 49.4
48	+ 27 4.5
49	+ 27 19.5
50	+ 27 34.6
51	+ 27 49.6
52	+ 28 4.6
53	+ 28 19.7
54	+ 28 34.7
55	+ 28 49.8
56	+ 29 4.8
57	+ 29 19.8
58	+ 29 34.9
59	+ 29 49.9
60	+ 30 4.9

Correction for MINS.

Mins.	Correction ° '
0	+ 0 0.0
1	+ 0 15.0
2	+ 0 30.1
3	+ 0 45.1
4	+ 1 0.2
5	+ 1 15.2
6	+ 1 30.2
7	+ 1 45.3
8	+ 2 0.3
9	+ 2 15.4
10	+ 2 30.4
11	+ 2 45.5
12	+ 3 0.5
13	+ 3 15.5
14	+ 3 30.6
15	+ 3 45.6
16	+ 4 0.7
17	+ 4 15.7
18	+ 4 30.7
19	+ 4 45.8
20	+ 5 0.8
21	+ 5 15.9
22	+ 5 30.9
23	+ 5 45.9
24	+ 6 1.0
25	+ 6 16.0
26	+ 6 31.1
27	+ 6 46.1
28	+ 7 1.1
29	+ 7 16.2
30	+ 7 31.2
31	+ 7 46.3
32	+ 8 1.3
33	+ 8 16.4
34	+ 8 31.4
35	+ 8 46.4
36	+ 9 1.5
37	+ 9 16.5
38	+ 9 31.6
39	+ 9 46.6
40	+ 10 1.6
41	+ 10 16.7
42	+ 10 31.7
43	+ 10 46.8
44	+ 11 1.8
45	+ 11 16.8
46	+ 11 31.9
47	+ 11 46.9
48	+ 12 2.0
49	+ 12 17.0
50	+ 12 32.1
51	+ 12 47.1
52	+ 13 2.1
53	+ 13 17.2
54	+ 13 32.2
55	+ 13 47.3
56	+ 14 2.3
57	+ 14 17.3
58	+ 14 32.4
59	+ 14 47.4
60	+ 15 2.5

Corr. for SECONDS

Secs.	Correction '
0	+ 0.0
1	+ 0.3
2	+ 0.5
3	+ 0.8
4	+ 1.0
5	+ 1.3
6	+ 1.5
7	+ 1.8
8	+ 2.0
9	+ 2.3
10	+ 2.5
11	+ 2.8
12	+ 3.0
13	+ 3.3
14	+ 3.5
15	+ 3.8
16	+ 4.0
17	+ 4.3
18	+ 4.5
19	+ 4.8
20	+ 5.0
21	+ 5.3
22	+ 5.5
23	+ 5.8
24	+ 6.0
25	+ 6.3
26	+ 6.5
27	+ 6.8
28	+ 7.0
29	+ 7.3
30	+ 7.5
31	+ 7.8
32	+ 8.0
33	+ 8.3
34	+ 8.5
35	+ 8.8
36	+ 9.0
37	+ 9.3
38	+ 9.5
39	+ 9.8
40	+ 10.0
41	+ 10.3
42	+ 10.5
43	+ 10.8
44	+ 11.0
45	+ 11.3
46	+ 11.5
47	+ 11.8
48	+ 12.0
49	+ 12.3
50	+ 12.5
51	+ 12.8
52	+ 13.0
53	+ 13.3
54	+ 13.5
55	+ 13.8
56	+ 14.0
57	+ 14.3
58	+ 14.5
59	+ 14.8
60	+ 15.0

This Table is to be used for both Stars and Aries.
The first full page column (Corr. for 1 hour + min.) is required
only when finding G.H.A. of a Star from G.H.A. ARIES
For Examples on the use of this Table see page 2:29 onwards.

Fig 81 Reed's Almanac 4:8.

Three Stars or Four?

In practice you might settle for the three-starred offerings. If faced with the RYA question, demanding two pairs at right angles, just plot the azimuths of all seven stars offered and make your selection. You might differ from the 'staff answers' but any reasonable choice is acceptable.

Will the Chosen Stars be Available Throughout Twilight?

This crafty question is easily answered. Look again at the extract from the Tables (Fig 79). Each degree change of LHA Aries is worth four minutes of time. Each block of figures gives 15 lines, so that is an hour. Actually, the sidereal time gives 15°03′ per hour, a trifling difference. So each star is available for at least one hour – Capella in the first column runs for three hours. However, if you took Capella at LHA Aries 43°, you only have eight minutes before it is replaced by Dubhe. But watch this trap: if you took Alpheratz at LHA 13°, for example, you might think it fades out in the next block, but it has simply moved to the right and lasts until LHA 74°. You will be safe if you allow 20 minutes either side as the RYA don't trouble with marginal cases.

Plotting Compound Sights

If you tackle these, either with standard plotting sheets or the latitude angle alternative, you need a system to avoid a muddle of lines. The plot shown (Fig 82) is three stars and the Moon. The RYA 'Ocean' course tends to give three stars and the Moon or a planet. Arrange a sensible scale for the longitude range covered. This is easy with the latitude/angle plotting sheet because the longitude scale will fit the heavy graph lines conveniently. I suggest a square box around the chosen position so you do not lose it. Draw the azimuth with broken lines so as not to confuse it with position lines, which you should first draw lightly. When a few of these have indicated the observed position you can firm up around it.

Precession and Nutation

Although the stars are gratifyingly stable in general, there are two small effects to account for. Precession is a top-like wobble of the Earth due to the effects of surrounding bodies. Nutation is a nodding motion superimposed on this for similar reasons. The precession and nutation cycle takes thousands of years to complete and

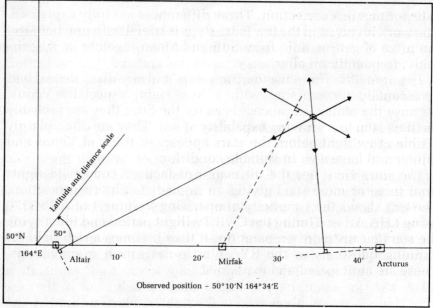

Fig 82   Multiple star sights.

the effects are small over a period of five years, which is the nominal
life of a given issue of Volume 1. Within this period, Table 5 (Fig 18)
gives a small correction by which the fix or position line is moved
bodily. Glance at the table and you will see whether the effect is
significant for your cruise.

Summary of Part Three

I believe this treatment of the Moon, planets and stars is intrinsi-
cally interesting and of special value to those taking the RYA Shore-
based Course on Astro-Navigation. Problem areas, well known to
instructors are identified and explained.

Parts One and Two have laid a firm foundation for the reduction
and plotting of sights, normally producing single position lines or
an observed position by Sun-Run-Sun. We have now extended this
to multiple sights capable of plotting a direct fix. This adds to the
fascination of the art and is a logical progression from the basic
capability aimed at in Part One.

The Moon Key points are that the lunar day is different; its
motion is wilder than for other bodies, and its comparative nearness

calls for parallax correction. These differences are fully explained. The work involved in the few extra steps is trivial with practice, and the prize of getting a fix from Sun and Moon together is, surprisingly, frequently on offer.

The planets The 'wandering stars' also offer themselves occasionally for crossing with a Sun sight, especially Venus. Because the reduction process is as for the Sun, they are probably the next step to a growing capability at sea. They are often plainly visible at twilight before the stars appear, so think of Venus and Jupiter and have a go in suitable conditions.

The stars Here lies the ultimate satisfaction: composite sights from three or more stars giving an immediate observed position. The text shows the simplicity of operating Volume 1 of A.P. 3270 using LHA Aries. Timing the Civil Twilight period and identifying the stars means more preparation. It thus becomes a rich field for cunning questions in the RYA's astro-navigation examinations. These are anticipated and explained.

Epilogue

Even if your dalliance with sextant navigation might be relatively brief and transitory, there is a quite significant time ahead through which it will provide comfort, support and intellectual stimulus. Arm yourself with a basic capability. Refer to the Sun sights review and summary of Part One as an *aide-mémoire* when necessary. Remember that you can lose Decca or Sat-Nav through no fault of the manufacturers – John Goode of Southern Sailing has experienced lightning strikes, which drove instruments mad, and a dismasting which was a very direct way of losing the antenna.

Think back to the lack of technical resources in 1767 when Charles II founded the Royal Observatory and briefed John Flamsteed to 'apply himself with most exact care and diligence to the rectifying of the tables of the motions of the heavens, and the places of the fixed stars, so as to find the much-desired longitude of places, for the perfecting the art of navigations'. So followed the Tables of Lunar Distances, and later the Summer Line and the St Hilaire Intercept method. If anyone had visualized satellite navigation at this time, he might have been treated like the Chinese astronomer who, in ancient times, got an eclipse prediction wrong . . . he was executed!

If you develop the capability this book aims at and feel you could have explained it better, then that is sufficient vindication for me.

Glossary

Altitude   Initially, the sextant angle of a body made with the visible horizon. Various corrections convert this to true altitude.

Amplitude   The true bearing of the sun at sunrise and sunset. Used as a compass check after applying variation.

Aries   A co-ordinate of celestial longitude used as the basis of star calculations.

Azimuth   The bearing of a heavenly body from the observer, or chosen position. Obtained from *Sight Reduction Tables*, or by calculator.

Celestial sphere   The convenient concept of an immense sphere with the earth at its centre and celestial bodies on its inner surface.

Chosen position   The smallest change from the yacht's area of uncertainty to a position catered for in the pre-computed Tables.

Circle of position   Part of a circle on which a yacht must lie as determined, usually, from horizontal or vertical sextant angles.

Dead reckoning   A yacht's position based on courses and distances run since the last recorded position.

Declination   The angular distance of a body north or south of the celestial equator. Treated exactly as terrestrial latitude.

Deviation   Deflection of the compass by magnetic influences within the vessel.

Dip   A negative correction to the sextant reading due to the height of eye above sea level. Easily treated in *Reed's* with other corrections.

Ecliptic   The apparent path of the Sun cutting the equinoctial at the spring equinox (Aries), and autumnal equinox (Libra).

Equation of Time   The connection between mean solar time, which is what we keep, and apparent solar time, which is what we observe.

Equinoctial   The great circle is the plane of the Earth's equator (equal days and nights).

Estimated position   Dead reckoned position with effect of tidal stream or current and leeway added. Both positions are loosely called DR.

GLOSSARY

Geographical position (GP) The point on the earth's surface directly beneath a navigational body. Expressed as declination and hour angle (latitude/longitude).

Gnomonic A chart projection giving great circle courses as straight lines. Also used for harbour plans and polar regions.

Great circle The shortest course between two points on the Earth. The savings over Mercator courses are significant over long distances.

Greenwich hour angle (GHA) The angle, measured westward, from the meridian of Greenwich to the meridian of the body (up to 360°).

Horizon The horizontal line marking the junction of sea and sky. The body is brought down to this (optically) when taking a sextant sight.

Index error The small residual sextant error, not sensible to adjust out. Checked before sight and noted 'on' or 'off' the arc for subsequent correction.

Intercept The measured difference between true altitude and tabulated altitude, along the azimuth from the chosen position. Can be 'to' or 'from' the body.

Latitude Parallels of latitude run up to 90° north or south of the equator, which is zero. The celestial equivalent is declination.

Local hour angle (LHA) The angle, measured westward, from the observer's meridian to the meridian of the body. Can be expressed in arc or time.

Longitude Meridians of longitude run 180° east or west of the Greenwich meridian, which is zero. The celestial equivalent is hour angle (up to 360° west).

Mercator The most common chart projection, in which declared courses cross meridians at the same angle. (Named after the famous cartographer.)

Micrometer drum The fine adjustment on the sextant, used after an approximate angle capturing the body has been found by de-clutching the worm drive.

Most probable position (MPP) A run-up from your past position to a newly found position line – the best you can do with a single position line.

Observed position The traditional way of describing a position obtained by astronomical sights.

Parallax A sextant correction of consequence for the Moon because of its nearness to earth.

Plotting The entry of courses and positions on charts and plotting sheets for the planning and execution of passages.

Plotting sheets Charts of a suitable scale, containing no land masses, for the graphical solution of sights. Can be fashioned from graph paper.

PZX triangle The spherical triangle formed by the elevated pole, the yacht's position, and the GP of the body.

Refraction Deviation of light rays by atmospheric effects. Calls for sextant correction and is greatest at low altitudes.

Rhumb-line A course on a Mercator chart, conveniently crossing meridians at the same angle. Not always the shortest over long distances.

St Hilaire Inspired inventor of the intercept method.

Semi-diameter A sextant correction for the Sun and Moon. We take the upper/lower limb for accuracy then correct to the centre.

Sextant The basic astro-navigational tool comprising a calibrated swinging arm and reflecting mirrors. It measures relative angles extremely accurately, normally between the horizon and the observed body. The design concept enables the required accuracy to be maintained despite the motion of a vessel in a seaway.

Sidereal Related to the stars. A sidereal day is 4 minutes shorter than a solar day and equals a day in a year.

Sight The process of observing and timing the altitude of a navigational body to establish a position line.

Sight reduction The processes of correction, and consideration of ephemeral data, required to establish a position line from raw data.

Sun-Run-Sun A morning sight for longitude, 'run up' by course and distance to the noon latitude sight; giving the daily position.

Tabulated altitude What the Tables reckon the altitude would have been from the chosen position at the time of sight. (Calculators work from DR positions.)

Twilight The 'shooting time' when the horizon and bodies are visible together. We aim for Civil Twilight – Sun 6° below the horizon.

Universal time (UT) Current usage for Greenwich Mean Time.

Variation Compass deflection caused by the Earth's magnetic field.

GLOSSARY

Zenith   An imaginary line from the Earth's centre passing upward through a point on the Earth's surface (directly overhead).

Zenith distance   The angle from the Earth's centre between the yacht and the GP of the observed body. Can also be quoted in nautical miles.

Zone time   Time differences from Greenwich based on one hour for each 15° of longitude. Used aboard for daily convenience and watch-keeping.

Index